**Designing Tomorrow:**
**The Architect's Guide to Sustainable Building Practices**

This comprehensive guide is an invaluable resource for architects, project developers and real estate investors who are committed to sustainable building practices. It provides a wealth of practical insights into cutting-edge materials and techniques, energy-efficient technologies and regenerative approaches to creating environmentally friendly, future-proof buildings. With detailed case studies and strategies, this book equips readers with the knowledge and tools to become leaders in sustainable architecture. Further books in this series are planned under the motto "**Transforming Real Estate through Architectural Expertise**".

by CW Wagener

# Table of Contents

# #01: Introduction to Sustainable Architecture

## The Importance of Sustainable Building Practices

Sustainable building practices are no longer an optional consideration but a fundamental requirement for architects and designers aiming to lead the way in modern construction. As the global community grapples with the pressing issues of climate change, resource depletion, and urbanization, the role of architects expands beyond mere aesthetics to encompass a responsibility for environmental stewardship. By adopting sustainable practices, professionals can significantly reduce the ecological footprint of their projects, ensuring that buildings contribute positively to their surroundings while meeting the needs of current and future generations.

Investors and real estate developers are increasingly recognizing the financial benefits of sustainable building practices. Properties designed with energy efficiency and environmentally friendly materials not only appeal to a growing demographic of environmentally conscious consumers but also command higher market values. Sustainable buildings often experience lower operational costs due to reduced energy consumption, making them more attractive to tenants and buyers alike. Moreover, many governments incentivize sustainable construction through tax credits and grants, further enhancing the return on investment for stakeholders who prioritize green building practices.

The integration of innovative technologies plays a critical role in advancing sustainable architecture. Smart home technologies enable real-time monitoring and management of energy use, allowing occupants to optimize their consumption patterns. Additionally, the use of biophilic design principles fosters a deeper connection between occupants and nature, promoting well-being and productivity. By incorporating these technologies into their designs, architects can create spaces that not only meet the functional needs of users but also contribute to a healthier urban environment.

Urban agriculture integration within sustainable design offers a unique opportunity to address food security and enhance community resilience. By incorporating green roofs, vertical gardens, and community gardens into building designs, architects can facilitate local food production while improving air quality and biodiversity. This approach not only promotes sustainable living but also strengthens social ties among community members, fostering a sense of ownership and pride in their environment. Such designs reflect a holistic understanding of urban ecosystems and the benefits they provide.

Finally, the principles of circular economy in construction must be embraced to mitigate the waste generated by traditional building practices. By prioritizing materials that can be reused or recycled, architects can significantly reduce the environmental impact of their projects. Furthermore, adhering to passive house standards enhances energy efficiency by utilizing design features that minimize energy loss. Eco-friendly renovation techniques ensure that existing structures can be upgraded sustainably, preserving cultural heritage while adapting to contemporary needs. Through these combined efforts, architects can pave the way for a sustainable future, demonstrating that responsible building practices are essential not only for the environment but also for the economic vitality of communities. In doing so, they foster long-term resilience in urban development, ensuring that buildings can adapt to future challenges. This holistic approach also strengthens community trust, as sustainable projects increasingly align with the social and ecological values of modern society.

## Current Trends in Architecture

Current trends in architecture are increasingly centered around sustainability and the integration of innovative technologies that address the pressing challenges of climate change and urbanization. Architects and building designers are now focusing on energy-efficient design strategies that not only reduce the environmental impact of their projects but also enhance the well-being of occupants. The adoption of green building materials is gaining momentum, with professionals seeking to implement solutions that minimize resource consumption and promote a circular economy. This shift is reflected in the growing availability of sustainable materials, which are often locally sourced and recycled, reducing the carbon footprint of construction processes.

One significant trend is the incorporation of biophilic design principles, which emphasize the connection between nature and the built environment. This approach aims to create spaces that foster well-being and productivity by integrating natural elements, such as plants, natural light, and water features, into architectural designs. As urban areas continue to expand, the need for green spaces becomes paramount. Architects are increasingly exploring urban agriculture integration, designing buildings that not only serve residential or commercial purposes but also provide spaces for food production. This trend not only contributes to food security but also enhances biodiversity and improves the overall quality of life in urban settings. Additionally, by incorporating vertical gardens and rooftop farms, architects transform underutilized spaces into productive areas that counter urban heat effects and reduce air pollution. Such innovations promote community engagement, as residents can interact with these green spaces and participate in urban farming initiatives. Ultimately, these nature-centric design approaches foster a more resilient, self-sustaining urban environment that prioritizes both ecological health and human well-being.

In tandem with biophilic design, smart home technologies are revolutionizing the way buildings operate. The integration of advanced systems that monitor energy usage, control lighting, and manage climate conditions allows for greater efficiency and user comfort. These technologies not only reduce operational costs for building owners but also align with the principles of sustainable urban planning by promoting energy conservation and reducing greenhouse gas emissions. Architects are tasked with designing spaces that seamlessly incorporate these technologies while ensuring they remain user-friendly and accessible.

Climate-resilient architecture is another critical focus area as communities face the growing threats posed by climate change. Building designs are increasingly incorporating adaptive strategies that enhance resilience to extreme weather conditions. This includes the use of materials and construction techniques that withstand flooding, heatwaves, and other environmental stresses. By prioritizing climate resilience, architects can ensure that their projects not only meet current needs but also withstand future challenges, thus providing long-term value to investors and real estate developers.

Lastly, the emphasis on passive house standards highlights the importance of energy efficiency in sustainable architecture. These standards advocate for designs that maintain comfortable indoor environments with minimal energy consumption, leveraging natural ventilation, insulation, and thermal mass. This approach not only reduces reliance on mechanical heating and cooling systems but also contributes to lower operating costs and a reduced ecological footprint. By focusing on passive strategies, architects can create resilient buildings that perform well in diverse climates and reduce long-term energy demand. Overall, current trends in architecture reflect a holistic approach to sustainable building practices, where the synthesis of innovative technologies, environmental stewardship, and human well-being drives the design of the future.

# The Role of Architects in Sustainability

The role of architects in sustainability extends beyond mere aesthetic considerations and functionality; it encompasses a commitment to environmental stewardship and social responsibility. As professionals tasked with shaping the built environment, architects are uniquely positioned to influence the sustainability of buildings and urban spaces. They can advocate for design strategies that minimize ecological footprints, optimize resource efficiency, and promote the use of renewable materials. By integrating sustainable practices into their projects, architects can significantly contribute to the broader goals of climate resilience and environmental preservation. Moreover, architects are pivotal in fostering community well-being by creating healthier, more adaptable spaces that support local ecosystems and encourage social cohesion. Through careful planning and design, they can reshape how cities interact with natural resources, reducing urban sprawl and conserving green spaces. Architects also play a key role in educating clients, stakeholders, and the public about the benefits of sustainable choices, promoting a shared commitment to environmental responsibility. In this way, they serve not only as designers but as advocates for a sustainable future, where architecture and nature coexist in balance.

Incorporating energy-efficient design into architectural practices is essential for reducing the operational costs of buildings while minimizing their impact on the environment. Architects can employ various strategies, such as passive solar design, natural ventilation, and high-performance insulation, to enhance energy efficiency. By adopting these strategies, professionals can create spaces that not only comply with stringent energy codes but also exceed them, providing long-term economic benefits for clients and users alike. Furthermore, as energy-efficient technologies continue to evolve, architects must stay informed and adaptable to incorporate innovations that can further enhance building performance.

The use of green building materials is a critical consideration for architects committed to sustainability. Selecting materials that are sourced responsibly, have low embodied energy, and are recyclable can significantly reduce the environmental impact of construction projects. Architects should prioritize materials that contribute to a circular economy, emphasizing reuse and recycling throughout the life cycle of a building. By specifying sustainable materials, architects can help foster a market that values ecological integrity and supports local economies, ultimately leading to a more sustainable construction industry.

Urban agriculture integration is another area where architects can make a substantial difference. As cities face increasing population densities and food security challenges, architects have the opportunity to design spaces that incorporate edible landscapes and vertical gardens. These features not only enhance the aesthetic appeal of urban environments but also promote biodiversity and community engagement. By creating multifunctional spaces that support urban agriculture, architects can contribute to healthier urban ecosystems and encourage a stronger connection between residents and their food sources.

Finally, the principles of biophilic design should be at the forefront of sustainable architecture. By emphasizing natural elements and fostering a connection between occupants and nature, architects can enhance the well-being and productivity of building users. Biophilic design can be seamlessly integrated with smart home technologies, allowing for environments that respond to the needs of occupants while maintaining energy efficiency. Incorporating features such as natural lighting, green walls, and water elements creates a sensory-rich environment that promotes mental and physical health. By embracing these principles, architects can create spaces that are not only sustainable but also nurturing, ultimately leading to healthier communities and a more sustainable future.

## The Role of Design in Sustainability

In today's world, where environmental concerns are at an all-time high, the role of design in sustainability has never been more crucial. Architects and designers have the unique ability to influence how buildings impact the environment, not only during construction but throughout their lifecycle. Sustainable design isn't just about using eco-friendly materials—it's a holistic approach that considers energy efficiency, resource conservation, and overall environmental impact.

Sustainable design begins with thoughtful planning. It's about integrating buildings harmoniously into their natural surroundings, taking advantage of natural light, airflow, and local climate conditions to minimize energy needs. By choosing materials with low environmental footprints and designing for durability and adaptability, architects can reduce the long-term ecological impact of a building. Passive design principles, like natural ventilation and solar orientation, further enhance sustainability, reducing reliance on artificial heating and cooling.

Beyond environmental benefits, sustainable design has social and economic advantages. Healthier indoor environments, often achieved through improved air quality, natural lighting, and better ventilation, enhance occupant well-being and productivity. Furthermore, energy-efficient buildings reduce operational costs over time, proving that sustainability and cost-efficiency can go hand-in-hand.

Designers also play a role in advocating for sustainable practices. By demonstrating the benefits of green buildings—both to clients and communities—architects can lead a cultural shift towards more responsible, sustainable construction practices. The choices made in the design phase have lasting effects, influencing not only the immediate surroundings but also setting a standard for future developments.

Importantly, sustainable design is not a one-size-fits-all solution. Every project offers unique challenges and opportunities, influenced by factors like location, function, and available resources. This calls for innovation, where architects employ emerging technologies—such as green roofs, rainwater harvesting systems, and renewable energy sources—to adapt to the specific needs of each site. By embracing flexibility and innovation, designers can create spaces that are not only functional and beautiful but also resilient in the face of climate change.

Sustainability is no longer optional; it's a responsibility. In the field of architecture and design, this responsibility manifests through intentional choices that prioritize the health of our planet and the well-being of those who inhabit it. Through sustainable design, architects have the power to shape a better future, one building at a time, and to inspire communities and industries to do the same

# #02: Green Building Materials

## Types of Sustainable Materials

In the pursuit of sustainable architecture, selecting the right materials is pivotal. Sustainable materials are those that minimize environmental impact while maximizing efficiency and longevity. They are derived from renewable sources, have low embodied energy, and can be recycled or repurposed at the end of their life cycle. Common categories include reclaimed materials, rapidly renewable resources, and materials that contribute to energy efficiency or indoor air quality. Understanding these types can guide architects and builders in making informed decisions that align with sustainable practices.

Reclaimed materials, such as salvaged wood, bricks, and metals, exemplify a commitment to sustainability by reducing waste and preserving resources. These materials often carry historical significance and unique character, contributing to a building's aesthetic while minimizing the carbon footprint associated with new production. Utilizing reclaimed resources not only promotes environmental responsibility but also supports local economies and craftsmanship. Architects who incorporate these materials can create spaces that tell stories and honor the past while addressing contemporary needs.

Rapidly renewable resources, including bamboo and cork, are another vital category of sustainable materials. These materials can replenish themselves quickly, typically within a few years, making them an excellent choice for projects aimed at reducing reliance on finite resources. Bamboo, for example, grows significantly faster than traditional hardwoods and can be harvested sustainably.

Similarly, cork, harvested from the bark of cork oak trees, regenerates without harming the tree, making it a renewable option for flooring and insulation. The integration of these materials not only enhances the sustainability profile of a project but also supports biodiversity and ecological balance.

Energy-efficient materials play a crucial role in reducing a building's operational energy consumption. Insulation materials, such as sheep's wool, cellulose, and recycled denim, provide excellent thermal performance while being eco-friendly. High-performance windows and solar-reflective roofing materials contribute to energy conservation by minimizing heat gain in warmer climates and heat loss in colder ones. By prioritizing energy-efficient materials, architects can design buildings that meet or exceed passive house standards, thus ensuring long-term sustainability and cost-effectiveness for occupants.

Finally, the concept of the circular economy in construction emphasizes the importance of materials that can be reused, recycled, or upcycled. This approach reduces waste and encourages a sustainable lifecycle for building components. Materials that are designed with end-of-life considerations in mind, such as modular systems and adaptable building components, allow for flexibility and longevity. Architects are increasingly called to embrace this mindset, ensuring that their designs not only respond to immediate needs but also adapt to future demands and challenges. By focusing on these types of sustainable materials, professionals can significantly impact the built environment and contribute to a more sustainable future.

# Sourcing and Certification of Materials

Sourcing and certification of materials is a critical component in the quest for sustainable building practices. Architects and design professionals must prioritize materials that not only meet aesthetic and functional requirements but also contribute to the overall sustainability of the built environment. This involves understanding the environmental impact of materials throughout their lifecycle, from extraction to disposal. By selecting responsibly sourced materials, architects can minimize resource depletion, reduce greenhouse gas emissions, and encourage ecological balance. The integration of local sourcing practices can also support regional economies and reduce transportation-related emissions, further enhancing the sustainability of a project.

Certification plays a vital role in ensuring that materials meet specific environmental standards. Various organizations offer certifications, such as FSC (Forest Stewardship Council) for wood products and Cradle to Cradle for a range of building materials. These certifications provide architects and builders with assurance that the materials used in their projects adhere to stringent environmental and social criteria. By leveraging these certifications, professionals can make informed decisions about the materials they select, ensuring that they contribute positively to sustainability goals. Additionally, transparency in the supply chain is paramount; architects should seek materials with clear documentation regarding their sourcing and production processes to verify compliance with sustainability benchmarks.

Incorporating green building materials also entails a thorough understanding of their performance characteristics, such as durability, energy efficiency, and the potential for reuse or recycling. Architects should evaluate materials based on their lifecycle assessments, which consider environmental impacts at every stage, from raw material extraction to end-of-life disposal. This holistic approach enables professionals to identify materials that not only reduce energy consumption but also enhance the resilience of structures against climate-related events. By integrating these materials into design practices, architects can create buildings that are not only aesthetically pleasing but also fundamentally sustainable.

Collaboration with manufacturers and suppliers is essential for architects aiming to source sustainable materials effectively. Building strong relationships with these stakeholders can facilitate access to innovative products that meet sustainability criteria. Many manufacturers are increasingly focused on environmental stewardship and are willing to share information about their sourcing practices, certifications, and performance data. By engaging in dialogue with suppliers, architects can advocate for transparency and sustainability, encouraging the broader industry to adopt responsible practices that align with the principles of sustainable architecture.

Ultimately, the successful sourcing and certification of materials require a commitment to ongoing education and awareness of emerging trends in sustainable building practices. Architects and building designers must stay informed about the latest developments in green materials, certification processes, and innovative technologies that support sustainability goals. By fostering a culture of continuous improvement and collaboration, professionals can not only enhance the sustainability of their projects but also contribute to the larger movement toward a more sustainable and resilient built environment. This comprehensive approach to sourcing and certification will ensure that future buildings are not only functional and beautiful but also aligned with the principles of sustainability that are critical for addressing the challenges of climate change and resource scarcity.

# Life Cycle Assessment of Building Materials

Life cycle assessment (LCA) of building materials is an essential tool for architects and designers committed to sustainable practices. By evaluating the environmental impacts associated with all stages of a building material's life—from raw material extraction through production, use, and eventual disposal—LCA provides a comprehensive understanding of the ecological footprint of various materials. This assessment enables professionals to make informed decisions that align with sustainable design principles while considering factors such as energy consumption, resource depletion, and greenhouse gas emissions. As architects and builders increasingly aim to create structures that are not only aesthetically pleasing but also environmentally responsible, LCA becomes a crucial component of the decision-making process.

In the context of sustainable architecture, the selection of building materials plays a pivotal role in minimizing environmental impacts. Materials like reclaimed wood, recycled steel, and low-VOC (volatile organic compound) products are gaining traction due to their lower life cycle impacts compared to traditional options. Through LCA, architects can compare the long-term benefits of these materials against their conventional counterparts, often revealing that sustainable materials not only reduce environmental harm but can also provide economic advantages over time. For investors and developers, understanding these benefits can lead to more profitable and sustainable building projects, enhancing property value and appeal in an increasingly eco-conscious market.

Moreover, LCA is instrumental in promoting the circular economy within the construction industry. By assessing the entire life cycle of materials, architects can identify opportunities for reuse and recycling, thus reducing waste and conserving resources. This approach aligns with the growing trend of eco-friendly renovation techniques and the integration of urban agriculture into building designs. For instance, the incorporation of green roofs or vertical gardens can enhance building performance while providing additional benefits such as improved air quality and biodiversity. Understanding the life cycle of these systems allows architects to design spaces that not only function efficiently but also contribute positively to their surroundings.

Climate resilience is another critical aspect where LCA can guide sustainable building practices. By analyzing the life cycle impacts of materials in relation to climate change, architects can select materials that withstand extreme weather events and temperature fluctuations. This foresight is vital for developing structures that are not only energy-efficient but also adaptable to future environmental conditions. The integration of smart home technologies further complements this approach, allowing for real-time monitoring of building performance and energy use, which can significantly enhance the sustainability of a project over its lifetime.

In conclusion, the life cycle assessment of building materials is a vital practice for architects, builders, and stakeholders seeking to advance sustainable design and construction. By embracing LCA, professionals can ensure that their choices contribute to a healthier environment while also meeting the demands of an evolving market. The transition toward sustainable materials and practices is not merely a trend; it represents a fundamental shift in how the construction industry approaches design, ultimately shaping a more sustainable future for urban development. Moreover, LCA empowers stakeholders to make data-driven decisions, aligning environmental impact reductions with economic efficiency. It also fosters innovation in material science, encouraging the development of low-carbon and circular economy solutions. As sustainability becomes a global priority, the widespread adoption of LCA will play a pivotal role in achieving long-term environmental goals and transforming the built environment.

# The Necessity of Construction Material Passports

Construction Material Passports are essential tools for advancing circular economy practices in the building industry. By documenting the composition, origin, and potential for reuse or recycling of materials, these passports enable efficient deconstruction, reduce waste, and preserve resources. They facilitate transparency across the supply chain, helping architects, builders, and recyclers make informed decisions that prioritize sustainability. As buildings serve as material banks, material passports ensure that resources can be recovered and reintegrated into future projects, driving long-term environmental and economic benefits.

# #03: Designing for Energy Efficiency

## Fundamentals of Energy Efficiency

Energy efficiency is a cornerstone of sustainable architecture, offering a pathway to not only reduce environmental impact but also enhance the economic viability of building projects. At its essence, energy efficiency involves using less energy to provide the same service or achieve the same outcome. For architects and building designers, this means implementing strategies that minimize energy consumption while maximizing comfort and functionality. By integrating energy-efficient design principles, professionals can create spaces that are not only more sustainable but also more appealing to investors and occupants.

Building orientation plays a pivotal role in passive solar design. Structures should ideally be oriented to capture maximum sunlight during the winter months while providing adequate shading in the summer. A south-facing facade typically receives the most direct sunlight, making it an excellent choice for incorporating large windows or glazing solutions. The right window placement can allow for natural light to penetrate deep into the building, reducing the need for artificial lighting during daytime hours. Moreover, designing overhangs or integrating shading devices can prevent overheating, ensuring a comfortable indoor environment throughout the year.

The implementation of energy-efficient design begins with a thorough understanding of a building's orientation, materials, and systems. Architects can leverage passive design strategies, such as natural ventilation, optimal daylighting, and thermal mass, to reduce reliance on mechanical systems. These strategies are central to the Passive House Standards, which prioritize air-tightness and insulation to create comfortable living environments with minimal energy use. Additionally, selecting green building materials that possess superior insulating properties can significantly enhance a building's energy performance, leading to lower operational costs and a reduced carbon footprint.

Smart home technologies further revolutionize energy efficiency in modern architecture. By incorporating automated systems for lighting, heating, and cooling, architects can design buildings that adapt to the needs of their occupants while optimizing energy consumption. These technologies not only enhance user experience but also provide valuable data that can inform future design decisions. As the demand for energy-efficient homes increases, investors and real estate developers are increasingly recognizing the importance of these features in attracting tenants and buyers, thus ensuring long-term returns on their investments.

The integration of biophilic design principles into energy-efficient architecture serves to create environments that foster well-being while minimizing energy use. By connecting occupants to nature through thoughtful design elements such as greenery, natural materials, and views of the outdoors, architects can enhance the psychological and physical health of inhabitants. This synergy between energy efficiency and biophilic design not only improves occupant satisfaction but also supports sustainable urban planning initiatives aimed at creating more livable, resilient cities.

In conclusion, the fundamentals of energy efficiency encompass a holistic approach that integrates design strategies, innovative technologies, and sustainable materials. For architects and building designers, embracing these principles is crucial in shaping the future of sustainable architecture. As

awareness of climate change and resource conservation continues to grow, the emphasis on energy efficiency will only increase, making it an essential consideration for all stakeholders in the
building industry. By prioritizing energy efficiency,
professionals can contribute to a sustainable future, ensuring that their designs are both environmentally responsible and economically viable.

# Passive Solar Design Strategies

Passive solar design strategies are essential for architects and building designers committed to
sustainability and energy efficiency. These strategies harness natural energy from the sun to regulate indoor temperatures, thereby reducing reliance on mechanical heating and cooling systems. By
maximizing solar gain in winter and minimizing it
in summer, passive solar design not only enhances
occupant comfort but also contributes to significant energy savings. Implementing these strategies requires a deep understanding of site orientation, building geometry, and local climate conditions, which are critical to optimizing solar exposure throughout the year.

Thermal mass is another crucial component of
passive solar design. Materials with high thermal

mass, such as concrete, brick, or stone, can absorb heat during the day and release it slowly at night. This characteristic is particularly beneficial in climates with significant temperature fluctuations between day and night. By strategically placing these materials in conjunction with sunlight exposure, architects can create a temperature-regulating effect that helps maintain a stable indoor climate. Additionally, incorporating thermal mass into the design can reduce energy costs by minimizing the need for heating and cooling systems.

Ventilation strategies further enhance the effectiveness of passive solar design. Natural ventilation can be utilized to promote airflow and cooling, relying on the principles of buoyancy and wind pressure. Designing buildings with operable windows, vents, and strategically placed openings can facilitate cross-ventilation, reducing the need for mechanical cooling. In warmer climates, incorporating features such as courtyards or green roofs can enhance air circulation and provide cooling effects, improving indoor air quality and occupant comfort.

In summary, integrating passive solar design strategies is a fundamental approach for architects and building designers aiming to create sustainable, energy-efficient structures. By focusing on building orientation, thermal mass, and ventilation, professionals can significantly reduce a building's energy consumption while enhancing the overall quality of life for its occupants. As the demand for sustainable construction continues to grow among investors and environmentally conscious individuals, mastering these principles will be key to leading the charge in the evolution of modern architecture.

## Integrating Renewable Energy Sources

Integrating renewable energy sources into building design is a pivotal aspect of creating sustainable architecture that not only meets current energy demands but also minimizes environmental impact. Architects and building designers must prioritize the seamless incorporation of solar panels, wind turbines, geothermal systems, and other renewable technologies into their projects. By embracing these energy sources, buildings can achieve significant reductions in greenhouse gas emissions while also enhancing their operational efficiency. The integration of renewable energy not only contributes to the reduction of energy costs over time but also positions a project favorably in the eyes of environmentally conscious investors and real estate developers.

Solar energy remains one of the most accessible renewable resources for urban and suburban developments. Designers can leverage both photovoltaic panels and solar thermal systems to harness energy for electricity and heating. Proper orientation and siting of buildings can optimize solar gain, while innovative design strategies such as solar canopies and green roofs can further enhance energy capture. It is essential for architects to collaborate with engineers to assess the feasibility of these systems early in the design process, ensuring that they are integrated effectively without compromising the aesthetic or functional aspects of the building.

Wind energy is another renewable source that can be integrated into building designs, particularly in areas with favorable wind conditions. Small-scale wind turbines can be installed on rooftops or within the vicinity of a building to supplement energy needs. Additionally, architects should consider the impact of building height, shape, and surrounding topography on wind flow to maximize energy generation. Incorporating wind energy solutions not only contributes to sustainability goals but also showcases a commitment to innovative, forward-thinking design, appealing to investors interested in cutting-edge technologies.

Geothermal systems provide an efficient means of heating and cooling buildings by utilizing the stable temperatures found underground. These systems can be particularly advantageous in climates with extreme seasonal temperature variations. Architects must consider the site's geological conditions and ensure that the design accommodates the necessary infrastructure for geothermal wells or loops. By integrating geothermal energy into the design strategy, architects can significantly reduce reliance on conventional HVAC systems, thus minimizing energy consumption and operational costs over the building's lifespan.

Finally, integrating renewable energy sources with smart technologies enhances energy management and efficiency. Smart home systems optimize energy use based on occupancy patterns and real-time data, while biophilic design principles reduce energy needs and enhance occupant well-being. By combining renewable energy, smart technologies, and sustainable design principles, architects can create resilient, efficient buildings that serve as models for the future of sustainable architecture.

# #04: Urban Agri-culture Integration

Urban agriculture represents a transformative approach to food production that integrates farming into the urban landscape, offering myriad benefits that resonate with sustainable building practices. By incorporating agricultural elements into city designs, architects and urban planners can enhance food security, reduce carbon footprints, and improve the overall quality of life for urban residents. This integration not only utilizes underused spaces, such as rooftops and vacant lots, but also fosters community engagement and resilience. As cities continue to grow, the incorporation of urban agriculture into architectural plans becomes a crucial consideration for sustainable urban development.

The environmental advantages of urban agriculture are profound. It can significantly reduce transportation emissions as food is grown closer to where it is consumed. This proximity minimizes the energy expenditure associated with transporting food over long distances, which is particularly relevant in the context of climate change. Furthermore, urban farms can contribute to biodiversity by creating green spaces that support wildlife, including pollinators like bees and butterflies. Such initiatives can also play a role in urban heat island mitigation, as vegetation cools surrounding areas and improves air quality, aligning with the principles of climate-resilient architecture.

From an economic perspective, urban agriculture can stimulate local economies by creating jobs and providing fresh produce to urban residents. Real estate developers and investors can tap into this trend by incorporating agricultural spaces into their projects, thus enhancing property values and attracting tenants who prioritize sustainability. Community-supported agriculture models can also foster direct relationships between producers and consumers, enabling residents to participate in the local food system actively. This not only provides a reliable source of fresh food but also strengthens community ties, which is essential for long-term urban sustainability.

Architects have a pivotal role in designing structures that seamlessly integrate urban agriculture. This may involve the use of innovative building materials that support green roofs or vertical gardens, which can be incorporated into residential and commercial buildings alike. Employing biophilic design principles, which emphasize the connection between people and nature, can enhance the aesthetic appeal of urban spaces while promoting ecological health. Additionally, smart home technologies can be integrated into these designs, allowing for efficient water use and energy management in agricultural practices, thereby maximizing sustainability.

In conclusion, the role of urban agriculture in cities is multifaceted and aligns with the broader goals of sustainable architecture. By implementing urban farming practices within their designs, architects and builders can contribute significantly to environmental sustainability, economic resilience, and social cohesion. Urban agriculture not only addresses food security but also transforms underutilized spaces into productive landscapes, fostering a deeper connection between residents and their environment. As the demand for sustainable living spaces continues to rise, the integration of urban agriculture will not only enhance the livability of cities but also serve as a model for future architectural endeavors that prioritize ecological balance and community well-being. By weaving green infrastructure into urban design, architects can redefine the relationship between cities and nature, creating spaces that thrive both socially and ecologically.

# Designing for Food Production

Designing for food production within urban environments represents a pivotal shift in architectural practice that aligns with the principles of sustainability and resilience. As cities continue to expand, the integration of food production systems into building designs not only addresses food security but also enhances community well-being. Architects must consider various methodologies to seamlessly incorporate urban agriculture, such as vertical gardens, rooftop farms, and community gardens, fostering a symbiotic relationship between built environments and food systems. This approach not only contributes to local food sourcing but also improves air quality and promotes biodiversity, making urban spaces more livable.

To effectively design for food production, architects should prioritize energy-efficient systems that support agricultural practices. This includes the implementation of smart irrigation technologies, greenhouse structures that maximize sunlight, and the use of renewable energy sources to power these systems. By applying biophilic design principles, architects can create spaces that are not only aesthetically pleasing but also conducive to plant growth. The incorporation of passive solar design elements, such as strategically placed windows and thermal mass materials, can significantly enhance the growing conditions for plants while reducing energy consumption in food production facilities.

The selection of green building materials plays a crucial role in creating sustainable food production environments. Utilizing locally sourced, sustainable materials can reduce the carbon footprint of construction while supporting the regional economy. Additionally, architects should explore innovative building techniques that promote circular economy principles, such as designing for disassembly and reusing materials. This not only minimizes waste but also allows for flexibility in adapting agricultural spaces as community needs evolve over time. By embracing these practices, architects can contribute to a more resilient urban fabric that prioritizes food production as a central element of sustainable living.

Integrating food production into urban planning necessitates collaboration with various stakeholders, including local governments, community organizations, and environmental advocates. Architects are uniquely positioned to facilitate this dialogue, ensuring that food production is woven into the fabric of urban landscapes. Sustainable urban planning should incorporate zoning regulations that support urban agriculture, as well as incentives for developers who commit to integrating food production in their projects. By advocating for policies that promote these initiatives, architects can help create a framework that encourages innovation and investment in sustainable food systems.

Ultimately, designing for food production is not merely an architectural challenge; it is an opportunity to redefine the relationship between urban living and agricultural practices. As architects and building designers explore these new paradigms, they contribute to a holistic approach that aligns with global sustainability goals. By focusing on energy-efficient design, smart technologies, and community engagement, the architectural community can lead the way in transforming urban environments into thriving ecosystems that prioritize food security, community health, and environmental stewardship. This integration of food production into urban design exemplifies a vision for the future where cities not only accommodate inhabitants but also nourish them.

# Case Studies of Successful Urban Farms

The integration of urban farms into city landscapes has emerged as a compelling case study in sustainable architecture, demonstrating the potential for multifunctional use of urban spaces while promoting environmental stewardship. One exemplary model is the Brooklyn Grange in New York City, which operates on rooftops across the borough. This initiative not only provides fresh produce to local communities but also serves as a green roof, enhancing insulation, reducing urban heat, and capturing stormwater. Architects involved in such projects can glean valuable insights into the integration of agricultural systems within urban environments, emphasizing the importance of designing structures that support biodiversity and contribute to overall ecological health.

Another noteworthy example is the Detroit Black Community Food Security Network, which has transformed vacant lots into productive urban farms. This initiative addresses food deserts while fostering community engagement and resilience. By employing permaculture principles, the design and layout of these farms maximize space efficiency and yield. Architects and planners can learn from the adaptive reuse of urban land, applying similar strategies to create green spaces that serve both ecological and social purposes. These case studies illustrate the importance of community involvement and local knowledge in the planning and design processes, ensuring that projects meet the specific needs of their surroundings.

In Toronto, the Everdale Farm exemplifies how urban agriculture can be seamlessly incorporated into educational frameworks. This farm not only produces organic vegetables but also serves as a learning hub for sustainable practices and environmental stewardship. The design principles employed here focus on accessibility and integration with the surrounding community. By prioritizing educational outreach and community involvement, architects can create spaces that extend beyond mere functionality, fostering a culture of sustainability that resonates with both residents and visitors. The incorporation of green building materials and energy-efficient systems further enhances the farm's role as a model for sustainable urban living.

The success of these urban farms highlights the role of circular economy principles in architecture and urban planning. By utilizing local resources and minimizing waste, these farms demonstrate how buildings can be designed to support regenerative practices. For instance, the use of reclaimed materials in construction and the implementation of water-efficient irrigation systems contribute to a sustainable ecosystem. Architects and building designers can draw from these examples to innovate within their projects, ensuring that every design decision contributes to a larger narrative of sustainability and resilience.

Ultimately, the case studies of successful urban farms underscore the potential for architects and developers to pioneer sustainable practices that reshape urban environments. By emphasizing biophilic design principles, urban agriculture can enhance the quality of life in cities, creating spaces that are not only environmentally conscious but also socially enriching. These projects serve as a testament to the ingenuity of integrating agricultural systems into the urban fabric, inspiring professionals to rethink the possibilities of urban design in the context of climate resilience and sustainability.

**Brooklyn Grange, New York City, NY**: Brooklyn Grange is one of the largest rooftop farms in the world. It spans over 5 acres across multiple rooftops in New York City. It produces over 50,000 pounds of organic vegetables annually. The farm also includes a green roof system that helps manage stormwater.

**DakAkker, Rotterdam, Netherlands**: DakAkker is a rooftop farm in Rotterdam. It grows food and helps to reduce flooding and support biodiversity. DakAkker is an example of urban spaces that combine food production with environmental resilience.

**Urban Organics, St. Paul, MN**: This aquaponics farm shows how urban spaces can be used for sustainable food production. It uses solar panels to power its operations and produces fish and greens for local markets, reducing the carbon footprint associated with food transportation. Urban Organics shows how urban farming can transform underutilized spaces into productive hubs for food and community.

# #05: Smart Home Technologies

## Overview of Smart Home Systems

The integration of smart home systems represents a transformative shift in how we approach residential design and construction. These systems leverage advanced technologies to create environments that not only enhance convenience and comfort but also promote energy efficiency and sustainability. By incorporating smart home technologies, architects and builders can significantly reduce energy consumption, streamline building management, and improve the overall quality of life for occupants. As we move towards a more sustainable future, understanding the role of these technologies becomes essential for professionals aiming to align their projects with modern ecological standards.

At the core of smart home systems are interconnected devices that communicate with each other and can be controlled remotely via smartphones

or centralized control panels. These devices include smart thermostats, lighting controls, security
systems, and energy monitoring tools. By utilizing
sensors and data analytics, smart home systems
can optimize energy usage based on real-time
conditions and user preferences. This not only
leads to reduced energy bills for homeowners but
also contributes to lower carbon footprints, aligning perfectly with the principles of sustainable
architecture and energy-efficient design.

The implementation of smart home technologies
also supports the circular economy in construction
by enabling more efficient resource management.
For instance, smart systems can monitor water
usage and detect leaks, significantly reducing waste in residential settings. Furthermore, they can facilitate the integration of renewable energy sources, such as solar panels, ensuring that energy
consumption aligns with production. This holistic
approach to resource management is essential for
achieving sustainability in modern architecture,
making it a vital consideration for architects and
developers alike.

In addition to enhancing energy efficiency, smart
home systems can contribute to the principles of
biophilic design by creating environments that
foster a connection between nature and technology. Features such as automated window shades

that respond to sunlight or smart irrigation systems that adapt to weather conditions can enhance indoor comfort while promoting ecological responsibility. This synergy not only elevates the user experience but also reinforces the importance of integrating nature into urban settings, aligning with sustainable urban planning initiatives.

As the demand for sustainable living spaces continues to rise, the market for smart home systems is expected to grow substantially. Investors and real estate developers are increasingly recognizing the long-term value that these technologies bring to residential projects. By prioritizing the incorporation of smart home systems, they not only enhance the appeal of their properties but also contribute to a more sustainable built environment. As architects and builders, embracing these innovations is crucial for designing tomorrow's homes that meet the needs of both occupants and the planet.

# Enhancing Energy Efficiency through Technology

Advancements in technology have become pivotal in enhancing energy efficiency within the built environment. Architects and building designers are increasingly integrating smart technologies into their designs, which not only optimize energy use but also improve the overall functionality of buildings. The adoption of Building Management Systems (BMS) allows for real-time monitoring and control of energy consumption. These systems can adjust lighting, heating, and cooling based on occupancy and environmental conditions, thereby significantly reducing unnecessary energy expenditure. As architects embrace these tools, they contribute to the creation of buildings that are not only more efficient but also more responsive to the needs of their occupants.

The use of energy-efficient materials is another critical aspect of improving overall building performance. Innovations in insulation materials, such as vacuum insulation panels and phase-change materials, provide superior thermal performance, minimizing heat loss and gain. This ensures that buildings maintain comfortable indoor climates with less reliance on mechanical heating and cooling systems. Furthermore, the integration of renewable energy technologies, such as photovoltaic panels and solar thermal systems, allows architects to design buildings that can generate their own energy. By utilizing these materials and technologies, architects can create structures that align with passive house standards, achieving net-zero energy consumption.

Urban agriculture integration into building designs exemplifies how technology can enhance energy efficiency while promoting sustainability. By incorporating vertical gardens and rooftop farms, architects can reduce urban heat islands and improve air quality. These green spaces not only provide fresh produce but also serve as natural insulation, further decreasing the energy needed for heating and cooling. The strategic design of these spaces can lead to innovative water management systems that utilize rainwater harvesting and greywater recycling, further emphasizing the role of technology in creating sustainable urban ecosystems.

Smart home technologies are revolutionizing how buildings interact with their occupants, offering unprecedented control over energy consumption. Home automation systems enable users to program their lighting and HVAC systems, optimizing energy use based on personal preferences and schedules. The integration of energy monitoring devices provides feedback that encourages occupants to adopt more energy-conscious behaviors. By designing buildings that incorporate these technologies, architects can foster a culture of sustainability among occupants, ensuring that energy efficiency becomes an integral part of daily living.

Finally, the principles of biophilic design play a crucial role in enhancing energy efficiency through technology. By creating spaces that connect occupants to nature, architects can improve mental well-being, which correlates with more sustainable building practices. Natural lighting, ventilation, and views of greenery can reduce reliance on artificial lighting and climate control systems. The use of technology to simulate natural conditions, such as circadian lighting systems, can further enhance these benefits. As architects embrace these holistic approaches, they not only enhance energy efficiency but also create environments that are healthier and more fulfilling for their occupants.

## Future Trends in Smart Building Solutions

The future of smart building solutions is poised to revolutionize the architecture and construction industries, aligning seamlessly with the growing demand for sustainable practices. As building designers and architects seek to create spaces that are not only functional but also environmentally responsible, the integration of advanced technologies will play a critical role. Smart building solutions harness data analytics, IoT devices, and artificial intelligence to optimize energy consumption, enhance occupant comfort, and improve overall building performance. These technologies enable real-time monitoring and control of systems such as heating, ventilation, air conditioning (HVAC), and lighting, leading to significant reductions in energy use and costs.

In the realm of materials, the trend towards sustainable building solutions is increasingly focused on the circular economy. Architects and builders are exploring innovative materials that not only reduce environmental impact but also support lifecycle sustainability. Reclaimed and recycled materials are gaining traction, as they help minimize waste and lower the carbon footprint associated with new construction. Additionally, advancements in green building materials, such as bio-based and high-performance products, are becoming essential components of smart buildings, allowing for enhanced energy efficiency and improved indoor air quality.

Urban agriculture integration is another promising trend within smart building solutions. As cities continue to grow, the need for sustainable food sources becomes paramount. Architects are beginning to incorporate vertical gardens, rooftop farms, and hydroponic systems directly into building designs. These features not only contribute to local food production but also enhance the building's aesthetic appeal and promote biodiversity within urban environments. By integrating agricultural elements into their designs, architects can create multifunctional spaces that foster community engagement and support healthy living.

The principles of biophilic design are also emerging as a fundamental aspect of future smart buildings. By incorporating natural elements and maximizing access to daylight and nature, architects can create environments that promote well-being and productivity. Smart building solutions can enhance biophilic design by utilizing adaptive technologies that respond to natural light and environmental changes, ensuring that indoor spaces remain comfortable and inviting. This connection to nature is increasingly recognized as essential for mental health and overall occupant satisfaction.

Finally, climate-resilient architecture is essential for the future of smart buildings. With the increasing frequency of extreme weather events, designers must prioritize resilience in their projects. Smart technologies provide predictive analytics to anticipate climate impacts and guide proactive design adaptations. Integrating renewable energy sources, such as solar panels and wind turbines, creates energy self-sufficiency, reducing dependency on vulnerable grid systems. Climate-resilient buildings can also include water management solutions like rainwater harvesting and green roofs to conserve resources. By embracing sustainable practices, architects can create buildings that not only withstand climate challenges but also contribute positively to the environment and communities.

Five Future Trends in Smart Building Solutions:

**AI-Driven Optimization**: Smart buildings will use AI to enhance energy efficiency, predictive maintenance, and real-time adaptability.

**Sustainability**: Emphasis on renewable energy, circular economy practices, and eco-friendly materials will dominate smart building design.

**Energy Resilience**: Advanced energy storage and efficient systems will improve sustainability and reliability.

**Occupant-Centric Design**: Buildings will prioritize health, comfort, and productivity through biophilic design and personalized environments.

**Smart City Integration**: Buildings will connect to smart city networks for data sharing and urban efficiency.

# #06: Biophilic De- sign Principles

## Understanding Biophilic De- sign: Fundamentals

Biophilic design emerges as a vital principle in sustainable architecture, emphasizing the intrinsic connection between humans and nature. This de- sign philosophy seeks to integrate natural ele- ments into built environments, fostering well- being, productivity, and a deeper appreciation of the natural world. By incorporating features such as natural light, vegetation, water elements, and organic materials, architects can create spaces that resonate with occupants on a psychological and emotional level. This connection not only enhan- ces the aesthetic appeal of a space but also cont- ributes to the overall health and happiness of its users, aligning perfectly with the goals of sustainable building practices.

The implementation of biophilic design can signi- ficantly impact the functionality of buildings. For instance, incorporating green roofs and walls can improve air quality, reduce urban heat, and promote biodiversity. These features offer a dual benefit: they enhance the building's aesthetic value while simultaneously addressing environmental challenges. Furthermore, access to natural light through well-placed windows and skylights can reduce reliance on artificial lighting, leading to lower energy consumption and costs. Such strategies illustrate how biophilic design principles can be seamlessly woven into energy-efficient design practices, creating spaces that are both functional and environmentally responsible.

Investors and real estate developers are increasingly recognizing the long-term value of biophilic design in their projects. Properties that embrace this philosophy often command higher market values and attract tenants who prioritize well-being and sustainability. As the demand for healthier living spaces grows, buildings that incorporate natural elements can differentiate themselves in a competitive market. Moreover, these designs can lead to lower vacancy rates and higher tenant satisfaction, ultimately resulting in better returns on investment. By aligning their projects with biophilic principles, developers can meet the evolving expectations of consumers while contributing to a more sustainable urban landscape.

Moreover, biophilic design plays a crucial role in promoting climate-resilient architecture. As urban areas face increasing environmental pressures, integrating natural elements can help mitigate the effects of climate change. For example, strategically placed trees and vegetation can provide shade, reduce heat island effects, and manage stormwater runoff. Additionally, these elements can enhance urban agriculture integration, allowing for food production within city limits and promoting local food systems. By fostering a harmonious relationship between the built environment and natural ecosystems, architects can contribute to resilient urban planning and sustainable community development.

In summary, understanding biophilic design is essential for architects and building designers committed to sustainable practices. This approach not only enhances the aesthetic and functional qualities of buildings but also promotes well-being and environmental stewardship. As the field of architecture continues to evolve, integrating biophilic principles will be key to creating spaces that resonate with occupants and foster a deeper connection to the natural world. By prioritizing these elements, professionals can lead the charge toward a more sustainable future, ensuring that architecture not only serves human needs but also respects and enhances the environment in which it exists.

Moreover, biophilic design contributes to long-term value by increasing occupant satisfaction and productivity, making it a wise investment for property developers and communities alike. In embracing nature-inspired solutions, architects can create resilient, adaptable spaces that respond to changing environmental and social needs, ultimately redefining the relationship between urban life and the natural world.

# Incorporating Nature into Architecture

Incorporating nature into architecture is an essential aspect of sustainable design, fostering a harmonious relationship between built environments and the natural world. This approach, often termed biophilic design, emphasizes the integration of natural elements into architectural projects, enhancing not only aesthetic appeal but also the psychological and physical well-being of occupants. Architects are increasingly recognizing that incorporating natural features—such as water elements, green walls, and abundant daylight—can significantly improve indoor air quality and reduce stress, ultimately contributing to a healthier living environment.

One effective method of incorporating nature is through the use of green building materials, which are sourced sustainably and often have a minimal environmental footprint. Utilizing these materials not only reduces the ecological impact of construction but also promotes a more organic aesthetic that resonates with the surrounding landscape. For instance, reclaimed wood, bamboo, and natural stone can be integrated into design schemes, providing both structural integrity and a connection to the earth. By prioritizing these materials, architects can create buildings that reflect their context while ensuring longevity and resilience.

Energy-efficient design plays a critical role in sustainable architecture, and natural elements can enhance these strategies. Incorporating large windows, skylights, and strategically placed overhangs allows for passive solar heating and cooling, reducing reliance on artificial lighting and climate control systems. Green roofs and living walls further contribute to energy efficiency by providing insulation and reducing the heat island effect in urban areas. By optimizing natural resources, architects can create spaces that are not only energy-efficient but also more sustainable over time.

Integrating urban agriculture into architectural projects is another compelling way to connect buildings with nature. Rooftop gardens, vertical farms, and community green spaces not only provide fresh produce but also foster community engagement. This approach not only addresses food security but also enhances biodiversity within urban settings. By designing spaces that accommodate urban agriculture, architects can promote sustainability while creating vibrant, multifunctional environments that enrich the urban landscape.

Finally, the principles of climate-resilient architecture hinge on the thoughtful incorporation of nature. By designing buildings that respond to their environmental context—such as using local materials, optimizing natural ventilation, and ensuring proper drainage—architects can mitigate the impacts of climate change. This forward-thinking approach not only protects investments but also enhances the longevity and adaptability of structures. Emphasizing the integration of nature in architectural design is not merely a trend; it is a necessity for creating sustainable, thriving communities that prioritize both human and ecological health. By fostering harmony between built environments and natural systems, architects can pave the way for a more resilient and balanced future.

# Benefits of Biophilic Spaces

Biophilic spaces are increasingly recognized for their multifaceted benefits, particularly in the context of sustainable architecture. By integrating natural elements into the built environment, these spaces not only enhance aesthetic appeal but also contribute to the well-being of occupants. Research indicates that exposure to natural light, greenery, and organic materials can reduce stress levels, increase productivity, and foster overall health. For architects and building designers, this presents an opportunity to create environments that prioritize occupant comfort while adhering to sustainable practices.

From an investment perspective, biophilic design has shown to be a key factor in increasing property value. Properties that incorporate natural elements tend to have lower vacancy rates and higher rental yields. Investors and real estate developers can leverage these trends to attract a discerning clientele that values sustainability and wellness. This can lead to long-term returns as demand for eco-friendly and health-oriented living spaces continues to grow in urban markets.

Moreover, biophilic design principles align seamlessly with energy-efficient practices. Natural ventilation, daylighting, and the strategic placement of

greenery can significantly reduce energy consumption in buildings. Architects can incorporate
these elements to create structures that not only
meet but exceed passive house standards. This
synergy between biophilic design and energy efficiency can enhance the overall sustainability of
projects, appealing to both environmentally aware
stakeholders and those focused on fiscal responsibility.

Urban agriculture integration is another vital benefit of biophilic spaces. By designing buildings that
incorporate green roofs, vertical gardens, or
community gardens, architects can promote local
food production while enhancing biodiversity. This
contributes to a more resilient urban ecosystem
and supports the circular economy in construction
by utilizing organic waste and promoting
sustainable practices among residents. Such innovations can attract environmentally conscious tenants and buyers, further increasing marketability.

Finally, biophilic spaces foster a sense of community and connection to the environment. By creating shared green areas and incorporating natural
elements into public spaces, architects can enhance social interaction and community engagement.
This is essential for sustainable urban planning, as
it encourages a sense of belonging among residents and promotes responsible stewardship of

the environment. As we move toward a future where climate resilience is paramount, integrating biophilic design principles into our architecture will not only improve human experiences but also strengthen our relationship with the natural world.

## Psychological and Social Aspects of Nature-Integrated Design

In recent years, architects and designers have increasingly recognized the profound psychological and social benefits of biophilic design—an approach that integrates elements of nature into built environments. In this chapter, we explore how incorporating natural features in design not only enhances the aesthetic value of a space but also supports mental health, fosters social interaction, and improves productivity. Research has shown that access to natural elements, such as greenery and daylight, can significantly reduce stress levels and improve overall well-being. By understanding these psychological and social aspects, architects can design spaces that are healthier, more engaging, and ultimately more sustainable. Furthermore, biophilic design fosters a deeper connection between people and their environment, encouraging a sense of stewardship and responsibility for the natural world.

## The Psychological Benefits of Nature in Architecture

Natural elements in design offer numerous psychological benefits to occupants, including reduced stress, enhanced mood, and greater cognitive function. Studies show that access to natural light, views of greenery, and the presence of organic materials like wood or stone can significantly improve mental health by triggering positive physiological responses. Some key psychological advantages of biophilic design include:

- **Reduced Stress and Anxiety**: Exposure to natural elements has been shown to lower cortisol levels, the body's primary stress hormone. This calming effect is beneficial in high-stress environments such as offices, hospitals, and schools, where mental well-being directly impacts performance and recovery.

- **Enhanced Focus and Productivity**: Biophilic design can improve focus and cognitive function, making it especially valuable in workspaces. Features like abundant daylight, indoor plants, and nature-inspired art help reduce mental fatigue and increase

productivity by mimicking natural environments that stimulate the brain.

- **Improved Mood and Well-being**: Access
to natural surroundings has a measurable
impact on mood and emotional resilience.
Spaces with biophilic elements tend to foster more positive emotional responses,
which contribute to a sense of well-being
and happiness among occupants.

## Social Aspects of Nature-Integrated Spaces

In addition to individual benefits, biophilic design
also supports social well-being and community
engagement. When applied thoughtfully, nature-
inspired spaces can encourage social interaction,
strengthen communal ties, and create a sense of
belonging within a building or neighborhood. Key
social benefits include:

- **Enhanced Social Interaction**: Common
areas with green spaces, water features, or
natural seating areas invite people to gather
and connect. For instance, urban parks,
rooftop gardens, and courtyards in office
buildings and residential complexes foster
opportunities for socializing and create a
shared experience that builds community.

- **Community Resilience**: Green spaces promote social cohesion by providing spaces for community events, group activities, and even gardening. This communal aspect of biophilic design is crucial in urban settings, where people often feel disconnected. When people share and maintain a space together, they feel more invested in their community, strengthening resilience and a sense of responsibility toward their environment.

- **Positive Influence on Behavior**: Natural settings have been linked to prosocial behavior, which is behavior that benefits others or society as a whole. People exposed to nature are more likely to exhibit cooperative, helpful, and empathetic behaviors, which can reduce conflict and improve overall social harmony within a building or community.

### Integrating Biophilic Elements for Psychological and Social Impact

Creating spaces that maximize these psychological and social benefits involves a strategic approach to biophilic design. Here are a few key design strategies:

- **Views of Nature**: Incorporate large windows, skylights, and glass walls to provide occupants with clear views of the outdoors. Even artificial elements, such as nature-inspired murals or digital windows that simulate natural views, can evoke positive psychological responses.

- **Natural Lighting**: Daylight plays a crucial role in regulating the body's circadian rhythms, which are essential for mental health. Use ample daylighting, light shelves, and smart window placement to maximize natural light while minimizing glare and heat.

- **Indoor Greenery**: Plants improve indoor air quality and bring a sense of vitality to spaces. Living walls, potted plants, and indoor gardens provide natural elements that can be particularly beneficial in dense urban environments where access to nature may be limited.

- **Water Elements**: Water features such as fountains or reflecting pools create a calming, soothing effect. The sound and sight of moving water can enhance relaxation and focus, helping occupants feel more connected to nature even in bustling urban environments.

**Biophilic Design Case Studies**

Case studies demonstrate how biophilic design can significantly impact occupants' psychological and social well-being:

- **Amazon Spheres (Seattle, WA)**: Amazon's corporate office includes biodome-like spheres filled with over 40,000 plants. Employees report feeling more relaxed, energized, and connected to their colleagues within this nature-rich environment.

- **School of Public Health (University of California, Berkeley)**: The school's integration of green roofs, native gardens, and ample sunlight improves student and staff well-being and provides a place for community interaction, fostering a positive academic environment.

- **Singapore's Parkroyal on Pickering (Asia)**: This award-winning hotel integrates extensive greenery, including sky gardens, waterfalls, and vertical walls, covering over 200% of its land area. The design promotes occupant well-being while reducing the urban heat island effect and enhancing biodiversity in the heart of the city.

- **Bosco Verticale, Milan, Italy (Europe)**: These residential towers feature vertical forests with over 20,000 plants and trees integrated into the façade, improving air quality and providing a natural aesthetic. The project demonstrates how biophilic design can blend urban living with ecological restoration, benefiting both residents and the environment.

- **One Central Park, Sydney (Australia)** One Central Park is an iconic example of biophilic design in action. Located in Sydney, this mixed-use development integrates vertical gardens that cover the building's facades, creating a living, breathing structure. Designed by Jean Nouvel and Patrick Blanc, the building features over 250 species of plants, fostering biodiversity in an urban environment. The green walls improve air quality, reduce the urban heat island effect, and provide a calming connection to nature. One Central Park demonstrates how biophilic principles can transform urban developments into sustainable, health-oriented spaces that reconnect people with nature.

# #07: Sustainable Urban Planning

## Principles of Sustainable Urban Development

Sustainable urban development is anchored in a set of principles designed to create resilient, livable, and environmentally responsible urban spaces. At its core, it emphasizes the integration of ecological considerations into the planning and design processes, ensuring that buildings and infrastructure not only meet the needs of the present but also safeguard the resources and environment for future generations. These principles advocate for a holistic approach that incorporates energy efficiency, sustainable materials, and innovative technology, guiding architects and builders towards creating spaces that harmonize with their surroundings.

One of the foundational principles of sustainable urban development is the emphasis on energy-efficient design. In this context, architects are encouraged to utilize passive design strategies that ma-

ximize natural light and ventilation, thereby reducing reliance on artificial heating and cooling systems. Incorporating renewable energy sources,
such as solar panels and wind turbines, further
enhances energy efficiency. By prioritizing these
methods, architects can significantly lower the
carbon footprint of their projects while providing
occupants with comfortable and health-conscious
living spaces. Moreover, integrating energy storage systems, like batteries, ensures a consistent energy supply even during peak demands or outages. This holistic approach not only reduces environmental impact but also enhances the resilience
and self-sufficiency of urban developments.

The integration of green building materials is another critical aspect of sustainable urban development. Utilizing materials that are locally sourced,
recycled, or sustainably harvested minimizes the
environmental impact associated with transportation and extraction. Moreover, these materials often contribute to better indoor air quality and
overall occupant health. Architects and designers
must remain informed about advancements in
eco-friendly materials, including those that promote circular economy principles, ensuring that their
projects are not only sustainable but also economically viable over the long term.

Smart home technologies play a pivotal role in enhancing the sustainability of urban environments. By implementing systems that optimize energy use, water conservation, and waste management, architects can create buildings that respond intelligently to the needs of their inhabitants. These technologies not only improve the efficiency of resource use but also provide valuable data that can inform future design decisions and urban planning efforts. Embracing such innovations allows architects to design structures that are adaptable to changing environmental conditions and user requirements.

Finally, the integration of biophilic design principles fosters a deeper connection between urban environments and the natural world. This approach encourages the incorporation of natural elements such as greenery, water features, and natural light into architectural designs, enhancing the aesthetic appeal and psychological well-being of occupants. Furthermore, urban agriculture initiatives can be seamlessly integrated into sustainable urban planning, transforming underutilized spaces into productive landscapes that provide food security and promote biodiversity. By adhering to these principles, architects and designers can contribute to the development of vibrant, sustainable urban areas that prioritize both ecological integrity and community resilience.

# Zoning and Land Use Conside-
rations

Zoning and land use considerations are critical elements in the planning and execution of sustainable building projects. Architects and building designers must navigate local zoning laws and regulations to ensure that their designs not only comply with existing frameworks but also foster sustainable practices. Understanding the nuances of zoning classifications—whether residential, commercial, or mixed-use—can significantly influence the potential for integrating green building materials and energy-efficient designs. As urban areas become increasingly dense, it becomes paramount for architects to advocate for zoning reforms that accommodate innovative designs and promote sustainability, contributing to long-term ecological health and community well-being.

Incorporating sustainable urban planning principles into zoning frameworks can help mitigate the impacts of urban sprawl, which often leads to increased carbon footprints and loss of green spaces. By promoting higher-density development and mixed-use areas, architects can create environments that encourage walking, cycling, and the use of public transportation. This not only reduces reliance on automobiles but also enhances community interaction and social cohesion. Further-more, the integration of urban agriculture within these zones can provide fresh produce, reduce food deserts, and foster biodiversity, aligning with the principles of sustainable architecture and en-hancing the quality of life for residents.

Investors and real estate developers play a crucial role in driving the adoption of sustainable prac-tices through their project choices. By prioritizing developments that comply with or exceed zoning regulations focused on sustainability, they can achieve long-term returns while minimizing envi-ronmental impacts. Projects that embrace passive house standards or utilize smart home technolo-gies often see increased market value due to gro-wing consumer demand for energy-efficient and environmentally friendly living spaces. Additional-ly, green-certified buildings frequently benefit from reduced operating costs, tax incentives, and access to favorable financing options, further en-hancing their financial viability. The alignment of economic incentives with sustainable practices not only benefits developers but also positions them as leaders in the evolving marketplace of green building, setting a benchmark for industry-wide transformation.

The circular economy in construction is another significant consideration in zoning and land use planning. Zoning codes should encourage practices that promote the reuse and recycling of materials, reducing waste and the demand for new resources. By facilitating the development of facilities that support material recovery and adaptive reuse, zoning can help architects and builders create projects that embody sustainability at their core. This approach not only conserves resources but also reduces the environmental footprint of construction activities, reinforcing the importance of sustainable practices in every phase of a project.

Lastly, climate-resilient architecture must be a priority within zoning and land use considerations. With increasing instances of extreme weather events, architects must design buildings that can withstand these challenges while minimizing vulnerability. Zoning regulations should encourage the use of green infrastructure, such as permeable surfaces and natural stormwater management systems, to enhance resilience. By collaborating with local governments to update zoning codes that reflect these needs, architects and stakeholders can ensure that future developments are not only sustainable but also capable of adapting to the changing climate, ultimately securing the well-being of communities for generations to come.

# Community Engagement in Urban Planning

Community engagement is a critical component of urban planning, particularly when considering sustainable building practices. Involving residents and stakeholders in the planning process ensures that developments reflect the needs and aspirations of the community. This participatory approach fosters a sense of ownership among residents, leading to more successful and sustainable outcomes. Architects and building designers must prioritize community engagement to align their projects with local values and expectations, which ultimately enhances the livability of urban spaces.

One effective method for engaging the community is through workshops and charrettes that facilitate open dialogue between designers and residents. These sessions can uncover local insights that inform sustainable practices, such as preferred green building materials or energy-efficient design features that resonate with community priorities. Furthermore, incorporating feedback from these sessions can lead to innovative solutions tailored to specific environmental contexts, ensuring that projects are not only architecturally sound but also environmentally friendly and socially responsible.

Investors and real estate developers also benefit from community engagement in urban planning. By understanding community needs and preferences, they can make informed decisions that enhance project viability and appeal. This engagement can lead to the development of mixed-use spaces that support local economies, ultimately driving long-term returns. Sustainable construction practices, when aligned with community desires, can create attractive living environments that increase property values and foster economic resilience, making the investment worthwhile. Moreover, projects that integrate green spaces and public amenities not only improve the quality of life for residents but also attract businesses and tourism, further boosting the local economy. By fostering transparent communication and collaboration with stakeholders, developers can build trust and gain public support, reducing potential opposition and delays. These efforts contribute to creating vibrant, sustainable communities that balance economic success with environmental and social responsibility.

The integration of sustainable urban planning principles is also enhanced by community participation. For instance, discussions around urban agriculture can reveal opportunities for incorporating green spaces and community gardens within developments. These spaces not only contribute to local food systems but also promote biodiversity and improve air quality. By actively engaging the community in these conversations, architects and developers can create designs that reflect a commitment to sustainability while addressing local environmental challenges.

Finally, the implementation of smart home technologies and biophilic design principles can be better tailored through community input. Residents may have unique insights into how technology can improve their quality of life or how nature can be integrated into urban settings. By fostering a collaborative environment where community voices are heard, architects can create resilient, climate-responsive designs that embody sustainable practices. This holistic approach to urban planning not only enhances the built environment but also strengthens community ties, ensuring that the future of urban development is both sustainable and inclusive.

# #08: Climate-Resilient Architecture

## Understanding Climate Resilience: Fundamentals

Understanding climate resilience is crucial for architects and building designers aiming to create structures that can withstand and adapt to the impacts of climate change. Climate resilience encompasses the ability of buildings and infrastructure to anticipate, prepare for, respond to, and recover from adverse climate events and conditions. This understanding is essential in a time when extreme weather events, rising sea levels, and changing climate patterns increasingly threaten urban environments and the communities that inhabit them. Architects must integrate resilience into their designs to ensure longevity, sustainability, and functionality in the face of such challenges.

At the core of climate resilience is the concept of adaptability. Buildings should be designed not only for their intended use but also to accommodate future changes in climate and occupancy patterns. This means considering design elements that allow for flexibility in space usage, such as movable partitions or modular components. Incorporating smart home technologies can further enhance this adaptability, allowing buildings to respond in real time to external environmental conditions. By focusing on these principles, architects can create spaces that remain useful and efficient, regardless of the climate changes encountered over time.

Another key aspect of climate resilience is the selection of appropriate materials and construction methods. Sustainable building materials, such as recycled, locally sourced, or rapidly renewable resources, can significantly reduce a building's carbon footprint while enhancing its durability. For instance, utilizing climate-adaptive materials that can withstand moisture or temperature fluctuations can prolong the lifespan of a structure. Furthermore, implementing energy-efficient design principles, such as passive solar heating and natural ventilation, contributes to a building's resilience by reducing reliance on nonrenewable energy sources and lowering operational costs over time.

In urban settings, architects must also consider the broader context of climate resilience within sustainable urban planning. This includes integrating green spaces, urban agriculture, and biophilic design principles that not only enhance the aesthetic value of a community but also improve its ecological health. Urban areas with ample green infrastructure can better manage stormwater, reduce heat island effects, and support biodiversity. Such designs can also foster a sense of community and well-being, which are vital components of a resilient society. Additionally, incorporating adaptive design elements, such as flood-resistant foundations and flexible-use spaces, ensures that urban developments remain functional during climate-related disruptions. By aligning urban planning with sustainability and resilience, architects contribute to creating cities that are prepared for future challenges while promoting environmental harmony and social equity.

Lastly, the transition to a circular economy in construction represents a paradigm shift that supports climate resilience. By prioritizing resource efficiency, waste reduction, and the reuse of materials, architects can contribute to a more sustainable building lifecycle. This approach aligns with passive house standards and eco-friendly renovation techniques, which emphasize energy efficiency and conservation. By designing buildings for disassembly and material recovery, architects can ensure that structures have a minimal environmental footprint even at the end of their lifecycle. As architects and building designers embrace these principles, they will not only enhance the resilience of their projects but also drive meaningful change toward a more sustainable and resilient future. This shift also creates new economic opportunities in the construction industry, encouraging innovation and the development of sustainable building technologies and practices.

## Designing for Extreme Weather Events

Designing for extreme weather events is a critical consideration in sustainable architecture, especially in light of the increasing frequency and intensity of such events due to climate change. Architects and building designers must prioritize resilience in their projects by incorporating design strategies that can withstand severe conditions, such as high winds, flooding, and intense heat. This involves not only selecting appropriate materials but also employing innovative structural techniques that enhance durability and minimize the risk of damage. Sustainable practices in this context involve understanding local climate patterns and vulnerabilities, thereby allowing for targeted interventions

that protect both the built environment and its occupants.

One effective approach to designing for extreme
weather is the integration of climate-resilient architecture principles. This includes elevating structures in flood-prone areas and utilizing materials that
are not only durable but also have low environmental impacts. For instance, materials such as recycled steel or sustainably sourced timber can offer strength and longevity while reducing carbon
footprints. The selection of energy-efficient design
elements, such as high-performance insulation
and energy-efficient windows, can also mitigate
the effects of extreme temperatures, thereby enhancing the overall comfort and safety of the building.

Urban agriculture integration emerges as a vital
strategy in this domain, particularly in urban settings that may experience food supply disruptions
due to extreme weather. By incorporating green
roofs, vertical gardens, and community gardens,
architects can create multifunctional spaces that
not only provide fresh produce but also contribute
to stormwater management and urban cooling.
This biophilic design principle not only fosters a
connection between occupants and nature but
also enhances biodiversity and promotes a

sustainable urban ecosystem, ultimately leading to more resilient communities.

Smart home technologies play a crucial role in enhancing the resilience of buildings against extreme weather. By incorporating systems that monitor and respond to environmental changes, such as automated shading devices or smart irrigation systems, architects can optimize energy efficiency and resource management in real-time. Additionally, integrating renewable energy sources, such as solar panels and wind turbines, can ensure that buildings remain operational even during power outages caused by severe weather. These technologies not only support sustainability goals but also provide a safeguard against the disruptions that extreme weather can cause.

Lastly, embracing a circular economy in construction is essential for fostering resilience in the face of climate challenges. By designing buildings with the future in mind, architects can create adaptable spaces that can be repurposed or deconstructed without waste. This approach encourages the use of eco-friendly renovation techniques and materials that prioritize longevity and recyclability. As investors and real estate developers increasingly seek sustainable construction practices, understanding the importance of designing for extreme weather events becomes paramount. It is an investment in not only the present but also the future, ensuring that buildings are capable of enduring the challenges posed by a changing climate while providing lasting value to communities.

# Innovations in Climate-Resilient Design

Innovations in climate-resilient design have emerged as a pivotal aspect of sustainable architecture, addressing the urgent need to adapt our built environments to the growing impacts of climate change. Architects and building designers are increasingly tasked with developing structures that not only minimize environmental footprints but also withstand the challenges posed by extreme weather events, rising sea levels, and shifting climate patterns. This evolution in design practices necessitates a comprehensive understanding of materials, techniques, and technologies that enhance resilience while promoting sustainability.

One significant innovation in this realm is the integration of green building materials that are both environmentally friendly and durable. These materials often include recycled components, local resources, and low-carbon alternatives, which can significantly reduce the overall carbon footprint of a project. Utilizing materials such as rammed earth, bamboo, or recycled steel not only contributes to sustainability but also ensures that structures can withstand local climate conditions. The selection process becomes critical; architects must prioritize materials that offer longevity and adaptability, reinforcing the idea that sustainable choices today will yield resilient buildings for tomorrow.

Energy-efficient design principles further bolster climate resilience. By incorporating strategies such as passive solar heating, natural ventilation, and high-performance insulation, architects can create buildings that require less energy to maintain comfortable conditions. This is complemented by the adoption of smart home technologies, which optimize energy use through automation and real-time monitoring. The synergy between energy efficiency and technological innovation not only enhances the comfort and functionality of spaces but also contributes to a building's ability to endure environmental stresses, ultimately delivering long-term value to investors and real estate developers.

Urban agriculture integration presents another innovative approach to climate-resilient design, particularly in densely populated areas where traditional green spaces are limited. By incorporating vertical gardens, rooftop farms, and community gardens into urban settings, architects can enhance food security, improve air quality, and create valuable green spaces for residents. This integration not only fosters community engagement but also plays a crucial role in mitigating urban heat effects and managing stormwater runoff. Such designs reflect a holistic understanding of sustainability that encompasses environmental, social, and economic dimensions.

Lastly, the principles of biophilic design are gaining traction as architects seek to create spaces that foster a deeper connection between occupants and the natural environment. By incorporating elements such as natural light, organic materials, and outdoor views, buildings become more attuned to their surroundings, promoting well-being and productivity. This approach aligns with climate resilience, as it encourages occupants to engage with and care for their environments, ultimately leading to more sustainable practices and community stewardship. Additionally, biophilic design can reduce energy consumption by utilizing passive cooling and daylighting strategies, supporting both environmental goals and operational cost savings. As cities become denser, integrating green spaces, such as rooftop gardens and indoor plant installations, provides critical access to nature within urban landscapes. This not only enhances the aesthetic appeal of buildings but also promotes biodiversity, offering habitats for urban wildlife. As the field of architecture evolves, embracing these innovations in climate-resilient design will be essential for professionals dedicated to building a sustainable future, creating spaces where people and nature thrive together.

Three Master Theses on Innovations in Climate-Resilient Design:

**Adaptability and Resilience:** Modular designs and durable materials enhance flexibility and longevity in the face of climate extremes.

**Resource Efficiency:** Integration of renewable energy systems and advanced water management reduces environmental impact and enhances self-sufficiency.

**Smart Technologies:** AI-driven systems enable predictive adaptations, safeguarding buildings and occupants against evolving climate risks.

**Community Integration:** Climate-resilient design fosters social cohesion by incorporating shared green spaces and disaster-preparedness infrastructure.

**Circular Economy Practices:** Designing for material reuse and minimizing waste ensures sustainable building lifecycles that align with long-term climate goals.

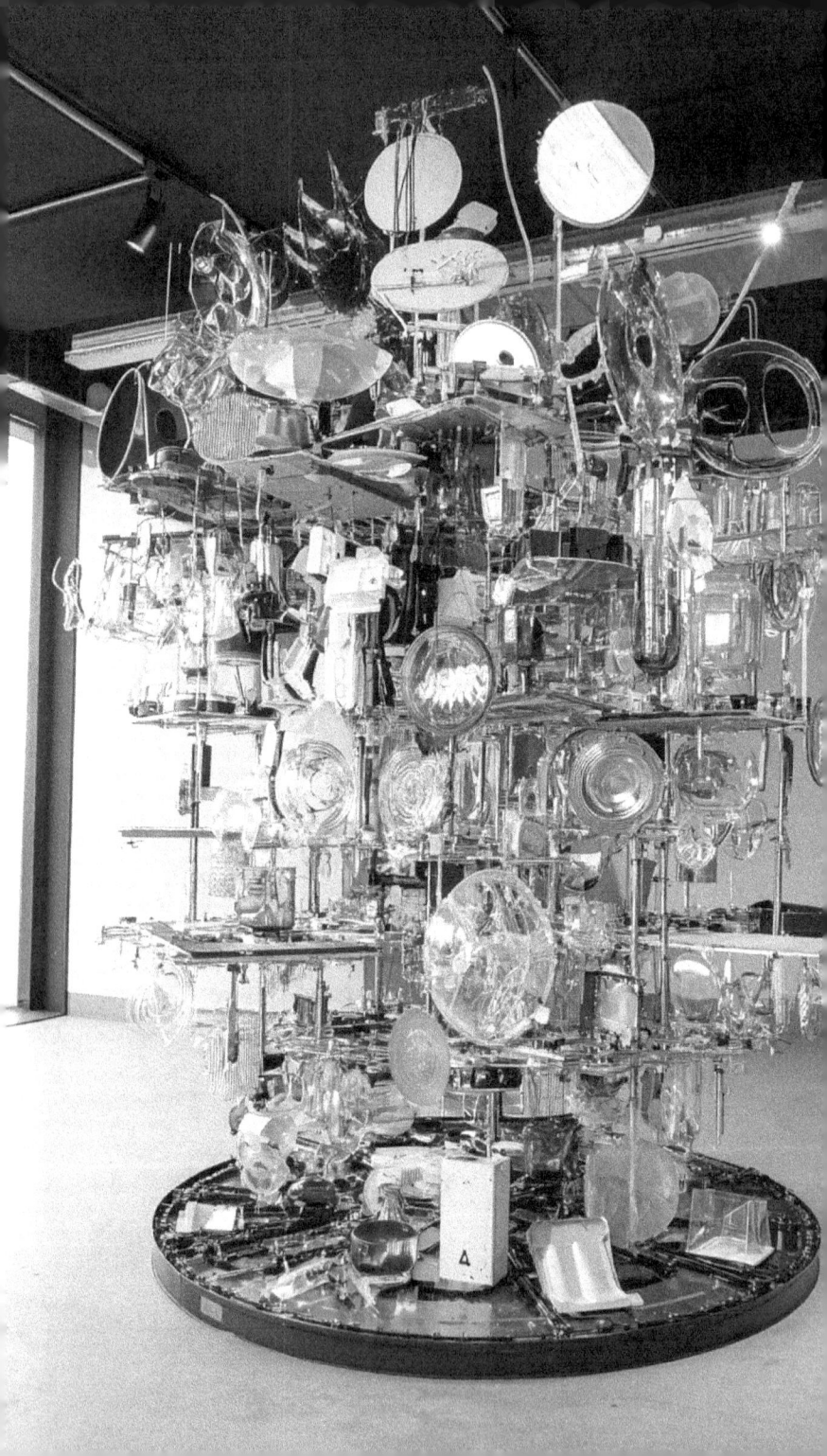

# #09: Circular Construction Economy

## Principles of Circular Economy

The principles of circular economy represent a transformative shift in how architects and building designers approach construction and design. At its core, the circular economy is centered on the idea of designing products and buildings to be restorative and regenerative by intention and design. This involves creating systems that minimize waste and make the most of resources through reuse, recycling, and sustainable practices. By adopting these principles, architects can significantly reduce the environmental impact of their projects while also enhancing the efficiency of resource use, leading to long-term benefits for both the environment and their clients.

One critical principle of the circular economy is the focus on resource efficiency. This involves optimizing material usage throughout the lifecycle of a building, from design and construction to operation and eventual deconstruction. Architects can implement strategies such as material selection that emphasizes renewable and recycled components, as well as designing for disassembly to facilitate future reuse. By considering the entire lifecycle of materials, architects can help ensure that buildings contribute positively to the environment rather than depleting it, thereby supporting sustainable development goals.

Another key aspect of the circular economy is the integration of systems thinking in design. This approach requires professionals to understand and analyze the interconnections between various elements of a building and its environment. By considering factors such as energy consumption, water usage, and waste generation holistically, architects can design buildings that operate efficiently and harmoniously within their ecosystems. This may involve incorporating smart home technologies that monitor and optimize resource usage, as well as integrating urban agriculture systems that not only provide fresh produce but also enhance biodiversity and promote community well-being.

Collaboration among stakeholders is essential for realizing the principles of the circular economy. For architects, this means engaging with clients, investors, and other professionals throughout the design and construction process to ensure alignment with circular economy goals. Investors and real estate developers can play a critical role by prioritizing projects that adhere to sustainable practices, ultimately driving demand for innovative solutions that align with economic and environmental objectives. Furthermore, fostering a culture of collaboration can lead to shared learning and the development of best practices that benefit the entire sector.

Finally, the circular economy encourages a paradigm shift in how success is measured in architecture and construction. Rather than focusing solely on profitability, there is a growing recognition of the importance of social and environmental impacts. Architects are increasingly called to demonstrate how their designs contribute to community resilience, environmental health, and overall quality of life. This approach shifts the narrative from short-term gains to long-term value creation, where buildings are designed to be adaptable, resource-efficient, and regenerative. By integrating innovative technologies and sustainable materials, architects can create structures that actively restore ecosystems and reduce waste. By embracing the principles of the circular economy, architects not only advance their profession but also become key players in creating a sustainable future, ensuring that the built environment supports both human and ecological well-being for generations

to come. This holistic perspective redefines architectural success, aligning it with global sustainability goals and societal progress.

## Strategies for Waste Reduction

Strategies for waste reduction in sustainable architecture are essential for minimizing environmental
impact while maximizing resource efficiency. Architects and building designers can implement a
variety of approaches throughout the design and
construction phases. By prioritizing waste reduction, professionals can not only enhance the
sustainability of their projects but also provide
added value to investors and real estate developers who are increasingly focused on long-term
returns through sustainable practices. This subch-
apter outlines several effective strategies that can
be integrated into architectural projects.

One of the most impactful strategies involves the
adoption of a circular economy framework in construction practices. This approach emphasizes the
importance of designing buildings and systems
that allow materials to be reused, repurposed, or
recycled at the end of their lifecycle. Architects can
collaborate with manufacturers who produce
sustainable building materials that are designed

for disassembly, facilitating the recovery of components and reducing landfill waste. By considering the entire lifecycle of materials from the outset, architects can significantly diminish waste generation during both construction and deconstruction phases.

Additionally, energy-efficient design plays a critical role in waste reduction. Implementing passive design strategies, such as maximizing natural light, utilizing thermal mass, and improving insulation, can reduce energy consumption and subsequently lower the amount of waste produced from energy generation. Incorporating renewable energy sources, such as solar panels, can further decrease reliance on non-renewable resources, contributing to a more sustainable building that aligns with the principles of climate-resilient architecture. By integrating these design principles, architects not only reduce operational waste but also enhance the overall efficiency of the building throughout its lifespan.

Urban agriculture integration offers another innovative strategy for waste reduction. By incorporating green spaces and community gardens into urban developments, architects can create systems that promote local food production and reduce the carbon footprint associated with transporting food. These initiatives can also help manage stormwater runoff and improve air quality, further aligning with sustainable urban planning principles. Engaging communities in these projects fosters a sense of ownership and encourages environmentally aware practices among residents, thereby amplifying the impact of waste reduction efforts.

Lastly, the use of smart home technologies can significantly enhance waste management in buildings. By implementing smart systems that monitor energy use, water consumption, and waste production, architects can help occupants make informed decisions that lead to reduced resource consumption. For example, smart appliances can optimize energy use based on real-time data, while smart waste management systems can guide users in sorting and recycling their waste effectively. These technologies not only streamline operations but also promote a culture of sustainability within communities, contributing to the broader goal of creating eco-friendly and resilient environments.

In summary, the strategies for waste reduction in sustainable architecture encompass a multifaceted approach that integrates circular economy principles, energy-efficient design, urban agriculture, and smart technologies. By adopting these practices, architects and building designers can contribute to the development of sustainable buildings that not only meet the needs of investors and developers but also advance the goals of environmentally aware stakeholders. Embracing these strategies is crucial for designing the future of architecture in a way that prioritizes sustainability and minimizes waste.

## Examples of Circular Practices in Architecture

Circular practices in architecture represent a transformative approach that prioritizes sustainability and resource efficiency throughout the building lifecycle. One notable example is the adaptive reuse of existing structures, where architects repurpose old buildings instead of demolishing them. This practice not only conserves materials and energy but also preserves cultural heritage, creating spaces that resonate with history while meeting contemporary needs. For instance, the Tate Modern in London, formerly a power station, has been successfully converted into a vibrant cultural hub, demonstrating how circularity can breathe new life into urban environments.

Another compelling example is the implementation of modular construction techniques, which allow for the design and assembly of buildings using prefabricated units. This method significantly reduces waste and construction time, as components are manufactured in controlled environments with minimal material loss. Projects like the Mjosa Tower in Norway, the world's tallest wooden building, showcase how modular practices can incorporate sustainable materials, enhance energy efficiency, and reduce the carbon footprint, all while meeting the growing demands for high-rise urban living.

The integration of biophilic design principles further exemplifies circular practices in architecture. By incorporating natural elements and promoting a connection to the outdoors, architects can enhance the well-being of occupants while improving energy efficiency. The Bosco Verticale in Milan, with its vertical forests, not only contributes to urban biodiversity but also helps to mitigate air pollution and improve thermal performance. Such projects highlight how embracing nature can lead to healthier living environments and promote sustainability within the urban fabric.

Sustainable urban planning also plays a crucial role in circular practices, emphasizing the importance of designing communities that prioritize resource sharing and reduce dependency on single-use systems. Projects like the Vauban district in

Freiburg, Germany, serve as models for eco-friendly urban development, featuring car-free zones, green roofs, and integrated urban agriculture. These initiatives foster a sense of community while maximizing the efficient use of resources, illustrating how holistic planning can lead to resilient and sustainable urban ecosystems.

Finally, the emergence of smart home technologies is revolutionizing the way buildings operate, making them more energy-efficient and responsive to environmental changes. Smart systems can optimize energy consumption, manage water resources, and enhance indoor air quality, all contributing to a circular economy in construction. The Edge in Amsterdam, often cited as one of the greenest buildings in the world, utilizes advanced technologies to monitor and adjust various systems in real-time, showcasing how innovation can align with sustainability to create spaces that are not only functional but also environmentally responsible. By leveraging data from sensors and IoT devices, smart buildings can anticipate and adjust to the needs of occupants, creating personalized environments that boost comfort and productivity. Additionally, these technologies allow for predictive maintenance, reducing waste by addressing issues before they become major repairs and extending the lifespan of building components. Integration with renewable energy sources, such as solar panels and battery storage, enables buildings to produce and manage their own energy more efficiently. As smart home technologies continue to advance, they offer a powerful tool for architects and developers seeking to build adaptable, sustainable spaces that respond dynamically to environmental and human needs.

# Design for Disassembly: Materials and Methods for Deconstruction

In the context of sustainable architecture, "Design for Disassembly" (DfD) is a critical approach that supports the principles of a circular economy by enabling buildings to be easily deconstructed at the end of their lifecycle. This chapter explores the strategies, materials, and construction methods that facilitate disassembly, promoting the reuse and recycling of building components. By integrating DfD principles, architects and builders can create structures that minimize waste, conserve resources, and reduce the environmental impact of demolition—a significant concern in the U.S. construction industry, where construction waste accounts for a substantial portion of landfill content.

Design for Disassembly is not just a sustainable building strategy; it represents a fundamental shift toward a circular economy where buildings serve as material banks for the future. By choosing materials and construction methods that facilitate disassembly, architects and developers can create structures that honor both the environment and economic sustainability. As the demand for sustainable construction grows, DfD will play an increasingly vital role in reducing the environmental impact of the built environment in the United States, setting a standard for responsible design practices.

## Understanding Design for Disassembly

Design for Disassembly is the practice of creating buildings in a way that allows for their parts to be dismantled and reused or recycled with minimal effort. This approach challenges traditional "build-to-last" principles, encouraging instead a "build-to-reuse" mindset. By making buildings adaptable and modular, DfD aims to extend the lifecycle of materials, components, and systems, reducing both the need for virgin resources and waste production. It enables a circular approach to construction, where materials can circulate back into new projects rather than ending up as landfill. Moreover, DfD supports resilience in the built environment by allowing structures to evolve and be re-configured as needs and technologies change over time.

The key principles of DfD include:

- **Ease of Disassembly**: Using connections and materials that simplify the separation of building components.

- **Modularity and Flexibility**: Creating standardized components that can be repurposed in future buildings.

- **Material Recovery**: Designing with materials that retain value and functionality after multiple uses.

## Benefits of Design for Disassembly

DfD offers several benefits that align with the sustainability goals of the circular economy:

- **Resource Conservation**: DfD reduces the need for raw materials by extending the life of existing ones, aligning with the U.S. goals to reduce reliance on finite resources.

- **Waste Reduction**: By enabling the reuse of building parts, DfD reduces the volume of waste sent to landfills, helping cities and states achieve waste reduction targets.

- **Economic Savings**: The reuse of building materials can lower costs for both demolition and new construction, making sustainable practices more financially feasible.

- **Environmental Impact**: DfD practices reduce greenhouse gas emissions associated with producing and transporting new materials, helping to mitigate the impact of the construction sector on climate change.

## Materials for Disassembly

Selecting materials suitable for disassembly is essential to ensuring the long-term success of a DfD approach. Key material considerations include:

- **Renewable or Recyclable Materials**: Prioritize materials like sustainably harvested timber, steel, and aluminum, which can be recycled multiple times without significant degradation.

- **Non-Toxic, Low-VOC Materials**: Avoid adhesives, paints, and finishes that emit harmful volatile organic compounds (VOCs) and cannot be easily separated from other materials.

- **Modular Components**: Use prefabricated elements like wall panels, floor tiles, and modular structural components that can be disassembled and reused with minimal modification.

## Construction Methods for Easy Disassembly

DfD requires specific construction techniques that allow for parts to be separated without damaging them. Effective DfD construction methods include:

- **Mechanical Fasteners over Adhesives**: Utilize bolts, screws, clips, and other mechanical fasteners instead of adhesives. These allow materials to be separated without causing damage, preserving the integrity of each component.

- **Modular Design**: Design structures using standardized, modular units that can be detached and reconfigured. This approach allows entire sections of a building, such as walls or floor systems, to be removed intact and reused.

- **Layered Building Systems**: Separate different building systems (e.g., structure, electrical, plumbing) into distinct layers that can be accessed and removed individually. This strategy prevents one system from interfering with the disassembly of another and allows for easier maintenance and up-grades.

- **Avoiding Composite Materials**: Composite materials, such as bonded wood and plastic, are difficult to separate and recycle. Instead, use materials that are either single-source or that can be dismantled into pure streams for easier reuse.

## Case Studies in Design for Disassembly

Several U.S.-based projects demonstrate the practical application of DfD principles. These case studies highlight the economic, environmental, and functional benefits of designing with disassembly in mind:

- **The Bullitt Center, Seattle, WA**: Known as one of the greenest commercial buildings in the world, the Bullitt Center incorporates modular interior components and separable building systems, allowing for eventual disassembly and reuse.

- **The Circular Building, New York City, NY**: This temporary structure was designed to be easily disassembled and reassembled elsewhere, demonstrating how modular design and non-toxic materials support reuse and recycling.

- **The Life Sciences Building, Portland, OR**: Utilizing materials like steel framing and prefabricated panels, this building demonstrates how commercial structures can be designed for disassembly without sacrificing functionality or aesthetics.

## Best Practices and Guidelines for DfD

Implementing DfD principles requires thoughtful planning and a commitment to sustainable building practices. Architects and builders can adopt the following guidelines to make DfD feasible:

1. **Plan for the Building's End-of-Life**: Consider the disassembly process from the beginning, mapping out how each component can be removed and reused or recycled.

2. **Choose DfD-Compatible Materials and Components**: Select materials that maintain value over time and can be easily dismantled, such as metals, solid wood, and natural fibers.

3. **Document and Label Components**: Create a detailed log of materials and components, labeling them with instructions for disassembly. This documentation ensures that

future owners or demolition teams understand how to dismantle the structure.

4.  **Collaborate with Manufacturers**: Partner
    with manufacturers who can supply com-
    ponents designed for reuse and provide
    take-back programs, where they reclaim
    used parts and recycle them.

## The Future of Design for Disassembly in the United States

The future of Design for Disassembly (DfD) in U.S.
construction looks promising as more cities and
states recognize the environmental and economic
benefits of circular building practices. DfD directly
addresses the need for sustainable resource management, aligning with growing awareness
around climate change and the construction sector's role in reducing carbon emissions. As the na-
tion moves toward stricter waste reduction targets
and higher sustainability standards, DfD offers a
tangible path for achieving these goals, providing
an efficient way to manage end-of-life building
materials by reintroducing them into the supply
chain rather than sending them to landfills.

The shift from a traditional construction model to
one focused on resource conservation will likely
be supported by regulatory incentives, making
DfD an attractive option for developers and inves-

tors. Cities such as San Francisco, New York, and Austin are already exploring policies that encourage or mandate sustainable building practices, including DfD, to reduce construction and demolition waste. Such policies could include tax breaks, grants, or streamlined permitting processes for projects that incorporate DfD principles. This regulatory push, combined with rising consumer demand for sustainable building practices, positions DfD as a valuable approach for developers seeking to meet environmental, social, and governance (ESG) standards and appeal to eco-conscious clients and investors.

Furthermore, advancing DfD practices aligns with the U.S. construction industry's movement toward modular and prefabricated construction, which naturally complements disassembly objectives. Modular components can be assembled with reusable connections, facilitating easy dismantling and reuse in new projects. Prefabricated systems are not only faster and more cost-effective to construct but also align with DfD by creating standardized, high-quality components that can be disassembled with minimal waste. This synergy between DfD and modular construction allows for flexible, adaptable buildings that can be expanded, reduced, or reconfigured as needs evolve, without compromising the integrity or usability of materials.

With innovations in materials science and construction technology, DfD will become a mainstream practice, transforming how buildings are designed, used, and ultimately, deconstructed. Advances in self-healing materials, biodegradable composites, and smart tracking systems—like embedded RFID tags to monitor the life cycle and location of each component—support a closed-loop model in which materials retain value over multiple lifecycles. These technologies not only make deconstruction easier and more efficient but also ensure that materials are correctly identified and diverted to appropriate recycling or reuse streams, maximizing the environmental benefits of DfD.

The future of DfD in the U.S. is one of collaboration, innovation, and environmental stewardship. As architects, builders, policymakers, and materials scientists work together, DfD has the potential to reshape the construction industry, shifting it from a linear, resource-intensive model to a circular, regenerative one. Ultimately, widespread adoption of DfD could lead to an industry where waste is a thing of the past, and buildings are viewed as material banks for the future, capable of adapting to changing needs and preserving valuable resources for generations to come.

In **Asia**, rapid urbanization drives the adoption of Design for Disassembly (DfD) as cities seek sustainable solutions to manage construction was-te. Countries like Japan lead in modular construc-tion and circular economy practices, incorporating DfD principles in earthquake-resistant, adaptable buildings. Singapore is integrating DfD into its green building standards, focusing on material re-covery and flexible designs to optimize land use.

In **Europe**, stringent environmental regulations and circular economy goals make DfD a priority. The EU promotes material passports and lifecycle assessments, ensuring resources are efficiently reused. Countries like Germany and the Nether-lands lead with modular and prefabricated sys-tems, exemplified by projects like the Circular Building in Amsterdam, which showcases fully di-sassemblable construction. Both regions demons-trate how DfD supports sustainability and resource conservation in diverse contexts.

# #10: The Passive House Approach

## Overview of Passive House Principles

The Passive House standard is an innovative approach to energy-efficient building design that emphasizes comfort, sustainability, and affordability. Rooted in a rigorous methodology, the principles of Passive House focus on minimizing energy consumption while maximizing user comfort. This framework is particularly relevant for architects and building designers aiming to create structures that not only meet current environmental challenges but also provide long-term economic benefits. By understanding and implementing these principles, professionals can contribute to a significant reduction in energy use and greenhouse gas emissions in the built environment.

One of the core tenets of Passive House design is the importance of superior insulation. Buildings must be constructed to minimize thermal bridging and air leakage, ensuring that energy loss is redu-

ced to a minimum. This involves using high-performance insulation materials and meticulous de-
tailing during construction to create a continuous
thermal envelope. For architects and builders, this
principle necessitates a shift in how walls, roofs,
and foundations are conceptualized and execu-
ted, allowing for more sustainable and resilient
structures that perform well in varying climatic
conditions.

Another critical aspect of Passive House principles
is the emphasis on airtightness. Ensuring that a
building is airtight not only enhances energy efficiency but also improves indoor air quality. This is
achieved through careful sealing of all joints, pe-
netrations, and connections within the building
envelope. For professionals in sustainable architecture, this principle highlights the importance of
integrating advanced building envelope technologies and conducting rigorous testing, such as
blower door tests, to verify performance. By prioritizing airtightness, architects can create healthier
indoor environments that contribute positively to
occupant well-being.

Passive solar design is also a fundamental component of the Passive House approach. By strategically orienting buildings and incorporating large,
high-performance windows, designers can harness natural sunlight for heating and lighting. This

principle encourages a thoughtful integration of passive solar strategies, which can include shading devices, thermal mass, and proper ventilation. For architects and building designers, this approach not only enhances energy efficiency but also fosters a deeper connection between occupants and their natural surroundings, aligning with biophilic design principles.

Finally, the use of high-efficiency mechanical systems is essential in achieving the Passive House standard. While the envelope plays a critical role in reducing energy demand, the integration of energy recovery ventilation systems ensures that indoor air quality is maintained without compromising energy efficiency. These systems recover heat or cooling from exhausted air, significantly reducing energy waste while maintaining a comfortable indoor climate. Architects and builders must consider these systems during the design phase to ensure that they complement the building's overall performance and meet rigorous Passive House criteria. Additionally, incorporating renewable energy sources, such as solar panels or geothermal systems, can further enhance the building's energy independence and sustainability. By embracing these Passive House principles, professionals can drive innovation in sustainable architecture, ultimately contributing to a more resilient and environmentally responsible future. This approach not only meets the demands of modern construction but also sets a precedent for achieving net-zero energy goals on a global scale.

# Benefits of Passive House Design

Passive House design represents a significant advancement in sustainable architecture, offering a myriad of benefits that resonate with architects, building designers, investors, and environmentally conscious individuals alike. At its core, Passive House principles prioritize energy efficiency through meticulous building envelope design, which minimizes heat loss and maximizes indoor comfort. This results in reduced energy consumption for heating and cooling, leading to significant cost savings over time. By integrating high-performance insulation, airtight construction, and advanced window technologies, architects can create spaces that maintain optimal thermal comfort with minimal energy input, appealing to both clients and investors focused on long-term operational savings.

In addition to economic advantages, Passive House design promotes a healthier living environment. The emphasis on airtightness and controlled ventilation systems ensures superior indoor air quality, which is vital for occupant well-being. By incorporating heat recovery ventilation, these homes not only maintain fresh air circulation but also recycle energy, further enhancing efficiency. For architects and builders, this commitment to occupant health aligns perfectly with the principles of biophilic design, fostering a connection between individuals and their environment. As society increasingly recognizes the importance of mental and physical health in our living spaces, the benefits of Passive House design in this regard become ever more compelling.

Moreover, investing in Passive House construction aligns seamlessly with the growing demand for climate-resilient architecture. As extreme weather events become more frequent, buildings must be designed to withstand these challenges while minimizing their environmental impact. The inherent energy efficiency of Passive House design significantly reduces greenhouse gas emissions, contributing to global sustainability goals. For investors and real estate developers, this translates to a forward-thinking approach that not only addresses immediate climate concerns but also positions their projects favorably within a market that values sustainability and resilience, ultimately enhancing property value and appeal.

Integration of smart home technologies within Passive House frameworks further amplifies its benefits. By utilizing automated systems for energy management, homeowners can optimize energy use, monitor consumption, and adjust settings to maximize efficiency. This synergy between Passive House design and smart technologies not only enhances user experience but also provides data-driven insights for architects and builders. Such innovations serve to future-proof buildings, ensuring they remain relevant and efficient as technology continues to evolve, making them attractive investments for developers looking to capture the market of eco-conscious consumers.

Lastly, the principles of the circular economy are inherently supported by Passive House design. By focusing on durable, sustainable materials and efficient construction practices, architects can minimize waste and promote resource efficiency. This approach not only benefits the environment but also aligns with the increasing demand for eco-friendly renovation techniques and sustainable urban planning. As the construction industry moves towards more responsible practices, embracing Passive House standards equips professionals with the tools to lead in this transformative era, ensuring that their projects are not only sustainable but also resilient and adaptable to future challenges.

# Certification Process and Guidelines

The certification process for sustainable building practices is a critical component of ensuring that design and construction meet established environmental standards. Architects and building designers must familiarize themselves with various certification programs such as LEED, BREEAM, and the Living Building Challenge, each offering distinct frameworks and criteria for sustainability. These certifications not only validate the environmentally friendly aspects of a project but also serve as a marketing advantage for investors and developers seeking to attract eco-conscious clients. Understanding the nuances of these certifications allows professionals to integrate them effectively into their project planning and execution.

To initiate the certification process, architects must first conduct a thorough assessment of their design concepts against the specific requirements set forth by the chosen certification program. This involves detailed documentation of energy-efficient designs, the use of green building materials, and sustainable site planning. A comprehensive approach should be taken, considering aspects such as water conservation, indoor environmental quality, and the overall lifecycle impacts of materials used. Engaging with sustainability consultants early in the design phase can streamline this process, ensuring that projects are aligned with the certification criteria from the outset.

Once the design is established, a series of performance metrics must be documented and verified to meet certification standards. This includes energy modeling, water usage calculations, and assessments of material sustainability. Utilizing smart home technologies can enhance a building's efficiency and contribute to meeting the stringent requirements of certification programs. Furthermore, architects should stay informed about the latest developments in sustainable practices, such as biophilic design principles and urban agriculture integration, which can bolster a project's ecological credentials and appeal to a broader audience.

The submission phase involves compiling all required documentation and evidence of compliance with the certification guidelines. This includes project plans, energy analysis reports, and documentation of materials sourced. A thorough review process by the certifying body follows, which may involve site visits and additional queries. Architects must be prepared to provide clarifications or adjustments based on feedback from the certification review team. This iterative process emphasizes the importance of attention to detail and a commitment to sustainability throughout the project lifecycle.

Achieving certification is not merely a checkbox exercise; it embodies a commitment to sustainable architecture and responsible building practices. For investors and real estate developers, certified projects often yield long-term financial benefits through operational savings and increased property value. Moreover, as awareness of climate change grows, the demand for sustainable architecture continues to rise, positioning certified buildings as desirable assets in the marketplace. By diligently navigating the certification process and adhering to established guidelines, architects can contribute significantly to the advancement of sustainable building practices, shaping a more resilient and environmentally friendly future.

## Certification Process and Guidelines in Europe

In Europe, sustainable construction certifications like BREEAM (Building Research Establishment Environmental Assessment Method) and DGNB (German Sustainable Building Council) set rigorous standards for environmentally responsible building practices. BREEAM, widely adopted across the EU, assesses projects based on criteria like energy efficiency, waste reduction, water management, and indoor environmental quality. The DGNB system, prominent in Germany and increasingly recognized throughout Europe, emphasizes a holistic approach that includes social, economic, and ecological factors, aligning with EU sustainability goals. Both certifications require detailed documentation, life-cycle assessments, and independent auditing to verify compliance with sustainability benchmarks. European Union regulations, such as the Energy Performance of Buildings Directive (EPBD), further reinforce these guidelines by mandating energy efficiency improvements in both new and existing buildings, supporting Europe's transition to a low-carbon, resource-efficient built environment.

## Certification Process and Guidelines in Asia and Australia

Sustainable building certifications in Asia and Australia emphasize energy efficiency, resource conservation, and environmental quality. Asia's **Green Mark Scheme (Singapore)** and **China Three Star Rating System** focus on climate adaptation and efficiency, while Australia's **Green Star** and **NABERS** prioritize carbon reduction and operational performance. These certifications ensure buildings meet sustainability benchmarks, enhancing resilience and market value.

# #11: Innovation and Future Trends

As the demand for sustainable and resilient buildings continues to grow, architects and developers are increasingly turning to emerging technologies and advanced materials to address environmental challenges and meet evolving building standards. In this chapter, we examine two main areas shaping the future of sustainable construction: cutting-edge materials and the role of artificial intelligence (AI) in building design and management. These innovations promise to redefine how buildings are constructed, maintained, and adapted to meet the needs of future generations. Advanced materials, such as self-healing concrete and carbon-sequestering building products, offer durability and environmental benefits that go beyond traditional materials, reducing maintenance costs and carbon footprints. Meanwhile, AI technologies enable buildings to operate intelligently, optimizing energy use, monitoring structural health, and even predicting necessary maintenance. Together, these advancements not only support sustainability goals but also improve buil-

ding performance, resilience, and the overall quality of life for occupants.

# Emerging Materials and Tech-
# nological Trends in Sustainable
# Construction

The construction industry in the United States is
embracing innovative materials designed to enhance sustainability, reduce environmental impact,
and improve building performance. From carbon-
neutral products to high-performance insulation,
these materials are paving the way for more eco-
friendly building practices. Key trends in this area
include:

- **Carbon-Neutral and Carbon-Binding Materials**: Traditional construction materials,
like concrete and steel, are significant cont-
ributors to greenhouse gas emissions. To
counteract this, new materials such as carbon-binding concrete, biochar-based products, and algae-derived bioplastics are
being developed. These materials not only
minimize the carbon footprint of buildings
but, in some cases, actively capture and

store carbon, contributing to climate change mitigation.

- **High-Performance Insulation and Thermal Management Materials**: Insulation
technology has evolved beyond fiberglass
and foam. Advanced materials like aerogels
and phase-change materials (PCMs) are
now used to enhance thermal performance,
reducing heating and cooling needs and
thus lowering energy consumption. PCMs,
for example, can store and release energy
as they change phases, providing natural
temperature regulation within buildings.

- **Biodegradable and Renewable Materials**: Biodegradable materials such as myce-
lium (mushroom-based materials), bamboo,
and cork are gaining popularity for their low
environmental impact and quick renewabili-
ty. These materials are particularly valuable
in applications where traditional building
products may leave a long-lasting environmental footprint.

- **Recycled and Reclaimed Components**:
The circular economy in construction encourages the use of recycled and reclaimed
materials, such as recycled steel, reclaimed
wood, and recycled aggregate in concrete.
Not only do these materials reduce the

need for virgin resources, but they also reduce waste, making them ideal for sustainable building practices.

- **Transparent Solar Panels and Building-Integrated Photovoltaics (BIPV)**: Transparent solar panels are an emerging technology that allows buildings to generate solar power from windows and facades without compromising aesthetics. BIPV, on the other hand, incorporates solar cells directly into building materials such as roof tiles or facades, making renewable energy generation a seamless part of the building's structure.

## Self-Healing Materials, Carbon-Sequestering Products, and AI-Driven Systems

As the construction industry looks to extend the lifecycle and sustainability of buildings, self-repairing materials, carbon-sequestering components, and artificial intelligence-based systems are emerging as transformative technologies.

Innovative materials and AI-driven technologies represent the future of sustainable architecture and construction in the United States. As the industry adapts to pressing environmental challenges, these advancements offer new pathways to reduce carbon emissions, enhance building resilience, and create smarter, more adaptive spaces. By embracing these technologies, architects, developers, and city planners can build for a future that prioritizes both environmental sustainability and occupant well-being. As these trends continue to evolve, they will undoubtedly shape the next generation of buildings, setting a new standard for sustainable design and resource management.

## Self-Healing Materials

Self-healing materials represent a groundbreaking advancement in building durability and longevity. Designed to repair their own damage, these materials reduce maintenance needs, extend building lifespan, and lower long-term costs:

- **Self-Healing Concrete**: Concrete is the most widely used building material globally, but it is susceptible to cracking over time. Self-healing concrete contains microcapsules of healing agents, such as bacteria or polymers, that activate when cracks form. These agents seal cracks and restore the material's integrity, enhancing the durability and reducing the need for frequent repairs, particularly in infrastructure projects.

- **Self-Healing Polymers and Coatings**: In addition to concrete, self-healing polymers and coatings are being used to protect surfaces and structural components from weathering and damage. These coatings, used in applications like steel beams and glass facades, can repair minor scratches and wear, preserving the visual and functional quality of buildings over time.

## Carbon-Sequestering Building Products

Carbon-sequestering materials are at the forefront of sustainable construction, actively capturing and storing carbon dioxide within building components. By integrating these materials, buildings can become part of the solution to climate change by serving as long-term carbon storage.

- **Carbon-Sequestering Concrete**: Innovations in concrete production are making it possible for this material to absorb and store carbon dioxide, rather than emitting it. Carbon-sequestering concrete uses additives that chemically bind carbon within the material, potentially storing carbon for the building's entire lifecycle.

- **Bio-Based Materials**: Biomaterials, such as hempcrete, algae-derived panels, and wood composites, naturally store carbon absorbed during plant growth. These materials are renewable, energy-efficient, and contribute to a building's overall carbon footprint reduction. They are especially valuable in applications where insulation, thermal regulation, and fire resistance are needed.

## Artificial Intelligence in Building Design and Management

AI-based systems are transforming the construction industry by enabling smarter, more efficient, and adaptive buildings. From the design phase through to building operation, AI applications are driving improvements in energy efficiency, predictive maintenance, and occupant comfort.

- **Design Optimization with AI**: AI algorithms can analyze vast amounts of data to optimize building design for energy efficiency, structural integrity, and aesthetics. AI-driven design tools, such as generative design software, enable architects to explore numerous design configurations, selecting options that maximize sustainability and performance. For example, AI can help determine optimal building orientation, window placement, and material choices for natural light and thermal efficiency.

- **Predictive Maintenance and Building Management**: AI-powered building management systems (BMS) monitor real-time data from sensors embedded throughout a building, allowing for predictive maintenance. This means potential issues, like HVAC inefficiencies or water leaks, can be detected and resolved before they lead to costly repairs or resource waste. Predictive maintenance reduces downtime and extends the lifespan of building systems, leading to more efficient and resilient buildings.

- **Occupant-Centric Controls**: AI also enables buildings to adapt to the needs of occupants. Through data analysis and machine learning, AI systems can adjust lighting, heating, and cooling based on occupancy patterns and environmental conditions, optimizing both energy efficiency and occupant comfort. AI-driven systems can also integrate with smart home technologies, allowing for seamless, automated control over building environments.

- **Smart Energy Management**: AI facilitates real-time energy management by analyzing energy consumption patterns and adjusting energy sources accordingly. For example, AI can optimize the balance between on-site renewable energy generation, such as solar power, and grid electricity, ensuring that buildings use the cleanest, most cost-effective energy available.

## Case Studies: Pioneering Projects Using Future-Ready Materials and AI Technologies

Several projects in the U.S. showcase how emerging materials and AI-driven systems are transforming sustainable construction:

- **The EDGE Building (Seattle, WA)**: Designed as one of the most energy-efficient office buildings, EDGE leverages AI-based systems for real-time energy monitoring, predictive maintenance, and occupant comfort control. The building integrates transparent solar panels and bio-based materials, setting new standards for sustainable design in commercial real estate.

- **The Savannah Hotel (Austin, TX)**: This hotel incorporates self-healing concrete in its foundation and walls, drastically reducing the need for maintenance in humid conditions. AI-driven building management monitors energy usage, water consumption, and indoor air quality, optimizing resource efficiency and guest comfort.

- **Urban Living Lab (Chicago, IL)**: This mixed-use development integrates carbon-sequestering materials, such as biochar-enhanced concrete and hempcrete walls, while using AI to manage the building's energy, lighting, and HVAC systems. The lab serves as a research and educational space, illustrating the potential of innovative materials and AI to redefine urban construction.

- **The Edge at Hudson Yards, New York City, NY**: This state-of-the-art building in Manhattan's Hudson Yards development integrates AI-driven systems to monitor and optimize energy use, temperature, and lighting, creating an adaptive, energy-efficient environment. The building incorporates advanced materials, including energy-efficient glass and low-carbon concrete, to reduce its environmental impact. AI technology tracks occupancy patterns, allowing the building's systems to respond in real time, adjusting HVAC and lighting to save energy while enhancing occupant comfort.

# #12: Eco-Friendly Renovation Techniques

## Assessing Existing Structures for Sustainability

Assessing existing structures for sustainability is a critical step in the journey toward achieving a more environmentally responsible built environment. Architects and building designers must begin by conducting thorough evaluations of current buildings to identify areas where sustainability can be integrated or enhanced. This involves analyzing the existing materials, energy systems, water usage, and overall efficiency of the structure. By employing tools such as energy audits and lifecycle assessments, professionals can gain a comprehensive understanding of the building's performance and its impact on the environment. The insights gathered from these evaluations can inform decisions about renovations and upgrades, ensuring that any interventions align with sustainable building principles.

A crucial aspect of this assessment is the evaluation of building materials. Many existing structures contain materials that are not environmentally friendly, contributing to a larger carbon footprint. It is essential to consider the potential for replacing or retrofitting these materials with sustainable alternatives. This not only improves the environmental performance of the building but can also enhance its aesthetic appeal and marketability. By embracing green building materials that are sourced responsibly and promote energy efficiency, architects can contribute to a circular economy in construction that reduces waste and maximizes resource utilization.

Energy-efficient design plays a pivotal role in the sustainability of existing structures. By examining the original energy systems, architects can identify opportunities for improvement, such as the integration of renewable energy sources like solar panels or the installation of advanced insulation techniques. Implementing smart home technologies can also significantly enhance energy efficiency, allowing for real-time monitoring and adjustments. These technologies not only reduce energy consumption but also provide occupants with greater control over their living environments, promoting both comfort and sustainability.

Sustainable urban planning must also be considered when assessing existing structures. The location and context of a building can greatly influence its sustainability profile. Architects should evaluate how the building interacts with its surroundings, including access to public transportation, green spaces, and community resources. Integrating elements of urban agriculture can also contribute to sustainability by promoting local food production and enhancing biodiversity. By designing projects that are not only sustainable on an individual building level but also within the broader urban landscape, architects can have a lasting impact on community resilience and environmental health.

Finally, implementing eco-friendly renovation techniques is vital for extending the lifecycle of existing structures while minimizing environmental impact. This approach prioritizes retrofitting and adaptive reuse over demolition, preserving the cultural and historical significance of buildings. Architects should advocate for passive house standards that emphasize energy efficiency and occupant comfort, ensuring that renovations align with the highest sustainability benchmarks. By fostering a culture of sustainable renovation, professionals can transform outdated structures into modern, efficient spaces that contribute positively to both the environment and the economy. In doing so, they support the shift toward a circular economy in construction, where resources are conserved and buildings are designed for longevity and adaptability.

## Green Renovation Strategies

Green renovation strategies are essential for architects and building designers aiming to enhance existing structures while promoting sustainability. These strategies encompass a range of practices that prioritize energy efficiency, resource conservation, and environmental impact reduction. By integrating sustainable materials and technologies into renovation projects, professionals can not only improve the performance of buildings but also align with the growing demand for eco-friendly practices among investors and occupants. A focus on green renovation enables architects to create spaces that are not only aesthetically pleasing but also functional and sustainable.

One effective strategy is the implementation of energy-efficient design principles. This involves retrofitting buildings with modern insulation materials, energy-efficient windows, and high-performance HVAC systems. Such upgrades reduce energy consumption and lower utility costs, providing significant returns on investment for developers. Additionally, utilizing renewable energy sources, such as solar panels, can further enhance a building's sustainability profile. By designing renovations that prioritize energy efficiency, architects can contribute to the reduction of greenhouse gas emissions and promote a healthier environment.

Incorporating green building materials is another critical aspect of green renovation strategies. Architects should consider materials that are sustainably sourced, recyclable, and low in volatile organic compounds (VOCs). For instance, using reclaimed wood, recycled steel, and non-toxic paints can significantly diminish the environmental impact of a renovation project. It is crucial to select materials that not only meet aesthetic and functional requirements but also contribute to the longevity and sustainability of the building. By championing the use of green materials, architects can lead the way in fostering a circular economy within the construction industry.

Urban agriculture integration presents a unique opportunity within green renovation strategies, especially in urban settings where space is limited. By designing rooftops and balconies for gardening and food production, architects can enhance building value while promoting local food sourcing. This practice not only supports community resilience but also enhances biodiversity and contributes to improved air quality. Integrating such features into renovation designs reflects a commitment to sustainable urban planning and encourages occupants to engage with their environment in meaningful ways.

Finally, the application of smart home technologies plays a crucial role in modern green renovations. These technologies can optimize energy use, enhance occupant comfort, and improve overall building performance. By incorporating systems such as smart thermostats, energy monitoring, and automated lighting, architects can create intelligent environments that adapt to the needs of their users while minimizing energy waste. Emphasizing these advanced technologies not only positions architects as leaders in sustainable design but also appeals to environmentally conscious investors and individuals seeking innovative living solutions. Through these green renovation strategies, architects can significantly impact the future of sustainable architecture and urban development.

# Case Studies in Eco-Friendly Renovations

Case studies in eco-friendly renovations illuminate the transformative potential of sustainable practices in existing structures. One notable example is the renovation of the Bullitt Center in Seattle, which has been dubbed the greenest commercial building in the world. This project exemplifies how integrating advanced energy-efficient design principles can revitalize an aging structure while maximizing its environmental performance. The renovation included solar panels, a rainwater harvesting system, and the use of local materials, showcasing a commitment to sustainability that not only reduces the building's carbon footprint but also serves as an educational tool for the community.

Another compelling case study is the retrofitting of the Bosco Verticale in Milan, which underscores the benefits of biophilic design principles. This residential project integrates urban agriculture by incorporating vertical gardens that enhance biodiversity while improving air quality. By prioritizing green building materials and energy-efficient technologies, the renovation has demonstrated how urban living can harmonize with nature. The success of this project illustrates how architects can push the boundaries of conventional design, creating spaces that foster both human well-being and ecological resilience.

The transformation of the historic Ford Assembly Plant in California into a mixed-use development provides insights into the circular economy in construction. This renovation focused on repurposing existing materials and structures, minimizing waste, and promoting sustainable urban planning principles. The project features adaptive reuse strategies that preserve the site's industrial heritage while incorporating modern amenities and energy-efficient systems. This case study emphasizes the importance of creativity and innovation in achieving sustainable outcomes, encouraging architects and developers to rethink the lifecycle of buildings.

In the realm of energy-efficient design, the renovation of the Kendeda Building for Innovative Sustainable Design at Georgia Tech serves as a benchmark. This project achieved net-positive energy status through its use of smart home technologies, including advanced building management systems that optimize energy consumption. The integration of passive house standards has ensured exceptional thermal performance, reducing reliance on mechanical heating and cooling. Such examples highlight the critical role of technology in facilitating eco-friendly renovations, providing a model for future developments.

Lastly, the restoration of the historic Smith House in Connecticut illustrates the application of eco-friendly renovation techniques in residential architecture. By implementing energy-efficient insulation, renewable energy sources, and sustainable landscaping practices, this project not only enhances the home's comfort but also minimizes its environmental impact. The case study of the Smith House reinforces the idea that sustainable renovations are achievable across various building types, encouraging architects and designers to adopt these practices in their own projects. As these case studies reveal, the future of architecture lies in our ability to transform existing spaces into sustainable, resilient environments that meet the needs of both people and the planet.

# Eco-Friendly Renovation Techniques in the European Context

In Europe, eco-friendly renovation techniques are essential for adapting existing buildings to meet modern sustainability standards while preserving the continent's architectural heritage. With a significant portion of Europe's building stock dating back decades or even centuries, the emphasis on renovation over demolition is strong, especially in densely populated cities where space is limited, and historical structures are valued. European policies and incentives, such as the European Green Deal and the Renovation Wave Initiative, are driving a shift toward sustainable retrofitting as part of the EU's strategy to achieve carbon neutrality by 2050.

Key eco-friendly renovation techniques in Europe include:

1. **Energy Efficiency Upgrades**: Retrofitting insulation, upgrading to energy-efficient windows, and installing modern heating and cooling systems are common practices. For example, Passive House (Passivhaus) standards, which originated in Germany, are often used in renovations to achieve high energy efficiency with minimal reliance on external energy sources. These renovations focus on airtightness, enhanced insulation, and the use of renewable energy systems like heat pumps or solar panels.

2. **Adaptive Reuse of Materials**: European projects frequently repurpose materials from the original building or other nearby structures. This reduces waste and minimi-

zes the need for new resources, aligning with the EU's circular economy goals. Salvaged materials, such as bricks, wood, and stone, are often carefully restored and integrated into renovations, preserving the building's historical character while reducing its environmental footprint.

3. **Sustainable Façade Renovations**: In historic buildings, the façade is often a defining feature. European eco-friendly renovation techniques focus on insulating and updating façades without compromising aesthetic or historical value. Techniques like interior insulation, ventilated facades, and green wall systems allow buildings to improve energy performance while maintaining their cultural significance.

4. **Integration of Renewable Energy Systems**: European regulations strongly encourage the installation of renewable energy systems, such as photovoltaic panels and geothermal systems, in renovated buildings. These systems not only reduce greenhouse gas emissions but also help owners comply with the Energy Performance of Buildings Directive (EPBD), which

mandates energy performance standards across the EU.

5. **Water Management and Green Infrastructure**: Many European cities prioritize water conservation and green infrastructure in renovations. Rainwater harvesting systems, green roofs, and permeable paving solutions are increasingly common in renovations to manage stormwater and reduce urban heat. Green roofs, in particular, help regulate building temperature, promote biodiversity, and enhance air quality, especially in urban areas.

Eco-friendly renovation techniques in Europe are supported by extensive subsidies and grants at both national and EU levels, making sustainable renovation an attractive option for building owners. By focusing on energy efficiency, resource conservation, and historical preservation, these techniques align with Europe's long-term environmental goals, creating resilient buildings that respect both the past and the future.

# #13: Designing Social Sustainability and Inclusion

Social sustainability and inclusion

Social sustainability and inclusion have become essential components of sustainable architecture, going beyond environmental goals to address community well-being, inclusivity, and social cohesion. In the United States, the design of buildings and neighborhoods increasingly considers social equity and community engagement as part of a holistic approach to sustainable urban development. This chapter explores strategies for fostering social interaction, promoting inclusivity, and creating welcoming public spaces that reflect and support the needs of diverse communities. By prioritizing social sustainability, architects and planners can help build neighborhoods that are not only environmentally resilient but also socially vibrant and inclusive.

Social sustainability and inclusion are indispensable elements of sustainable design, fostering a sense of community, equity, and resilience in buildings and public spaces across the United States. By promoting social interaction, designing inclusive environments, and involving communities in planning, architects and urban planners can create spaces that reflect the diverse needs of their users. As cities continue to grow and evolve, prioritizing social sustainability will be key to building neighborhoods that are not only environmentally responsible but also socially cohesive, vibrant, and accessible for all. Inclusive design can help bridge socioeconomic gaps by creating public spaces that welcome people of all backgrounds, encouraging diverse communities to come together. This approach also supports mental health and well-being, as inclusive, well-designed environments contribute to a sense of belonging and personal investment in shared spaces. Furthermore, inclusive public spaces provide opportunities for cultural expression and celebrate diversity, strengthening community identity. Ultimately, socially sustainable design strengthens communities, making them more resilient to challenges and enhancing quality of life for residents. This focus on social sustainability also boosts local economies, as vibrant, inclusive spaces attract both residents and visitors, creating a thriving community fabric.

# Promoting Social Interaction and Inclusivity in Sustainable Buildings and Neighborhoods

Sustainable buildings and neighborhoods are designed not only to minimize environmental impact but also to foster social interaction, inclusivity, and a sense of belonging among residents. The built environment plays a critical role in shaping how people interact, making it essential for architects and urban planners to design spaces that encourage connection and community.

- **Creating Communal Spaces**: Well-designed communal spaces–such as shared courtyards, rooftop gardens, and co-working lounges–offer opportunities for residents to connect and interact. In multi-family housing, for instance, shared green spaces and community kitchens create focal points for socializing and allow residents to form bonds, supporting a stronger sense of community.

- **Inclusive Design Features**: Inclusive design aims to create spaces that are accessible and welcoming to everyone, regardless of age, ability, or background. Features like universal design principles, ADA-compliant ramps and elevators, tactile paving for the visually impaired, and multi-sensory installations cater to a wide range of abilities and preferences. Incorporating these elements makes buildings more accessible, fostering inclusivity and ensuring that all individuals can navigate and enjoy shared spaces.

- **Affordable Housing and Mixed-Income Communities**: Social sustainability also involves addressing economic inclusion by incorporating affordable housing within sustainable developments. Mixed-income communities reduce segregation and promote economic diversity, enabling people from various backgrounds to live and interact together. For example, cities like New York and San Francisco have integrated affordable housing mandates within new developments, fostering inclusive communities that reflect the socioeconomic diversity of their regions.

- **Programming for Social Engagement**: Active programming, such as community events, educational workshops, and cultural festivals, can also enhance social interaction. For example, urban farms or community gardens within residential areas create spaces for shared activities and learning, where residents can work together, exch- ange knowledge, and create a sense of community ownership. Events like farmers' markets, outdoor movie nights, or fitness classes hosted within common areas further encourage residents to engage with one another.

# Engaging Communities and Creating Inclusive Public Spaces

Public spaces play a vital role in building socially inclusive cities by providing accessible, welcoming environments where people can come together and interact. Designing these spaces with a focus on inclusivity and community engagement can lead to more cohesive neighborhoods, vibrant lo- cal economies, and increased civic pride.Public spaces play a vital role in building socially inclusi- ve cities by providing accessible, welcoming envi- ronments where people can come together and interact. Designing these spaces with a focus on inclusivity and community engagement can lead to more cohesive neighborhoods, vibrant local economies, and increased civic pride. Inclusive public spaces offer opportunities for diverse cultural expressions, community events, and local markets, which can foster a sense of identity and shared purpose. When public spaces are thoughtfully designed, they encourage social interactions among people of different ages, backgrounds, and abilities, strengthening community bonds. Additionally, accessible green spaces and recreational areas contribute to public health and well-being, making neighborhoods more livable and attractive for residents and visitors alike.

- **Designing Inclusive Public Spaces**: Inclusive public spaces consider the needs of diverse users, creating environments that are safe, welcoming, and accessible to people from all backgrounds and abilities. Parks with wheelchair-accessible paths, seating designed for people of all ages, gender-neutral restrooms, and sensory-friendly areas create public spaces that cater to everyone. For example, New York City's High Line park features accessible ramps, frequent seating, and open sightlines, making it easy for people with diverse needs to navigate and enjoy.

- **Community-Led Planning and Engagement**: Community engagement is essential in the design of inclusive public spaces. By involving residents in the planning and design process, architects and city planners can better understand the needs, values, and priorities of the community. This could involve participatory design workshops, focus groups, or community surveys that allow residents to share their ideas and provide input on the layout, features, and programming of new public spaces. Community-led planning has proven effective in cities like Detroit, where residents have been involved in the revitalization of parks and public spaces, ensuring that these areas reflect local culture and meet the needs of the community.

- **Equity in Access to Public Amenities**: Social sustainability also entails equitable access to public amenities like parks, recreation centers, and libraries. Ensuring that underserved neighborhoods have equal access to high-quality public spaces helps reduce disparities and promotes a more inclusive urban environment. For example, Los Angeles has prioritized investments in public parks and recreational facilities in low-income neighborhoods, addressing inequities in access to green spaces and enhancing social cohesion.

- **Place-Making and Cultural Expression**: Inclusive public spaces can also serve as platforms for cultural expression, where communities can celebrate their heritage and traditions. Place-making initiatives that incorporate local art, murals, and installations provide a sense of ownership and pride among residents. Projects like San Francisco's Mission District murals or Chicago's community art in Pilsen reflect the cultural identity of these neighborhoods, allowing residents to engage with and contribute to the visual landscape of their community.

- **Flexible and Adaptive Spaces**: The design of adaptable and flexible public spaces allows them to evolve with the needs of the community over time. For example, open-air plazas or modular pavilions can be used for markets, exhibitions, or performances, while still serving as places for casual gatherings when not in use. Adaptable design promotes the long-term viability of public spaces, making them responsive to changing demographics and community interests.

# Case Studies: Socially Sustainable and Inclusive Projects

Several projects in the United States exemplify successful approaches to social sustainability and inclusion in the built environment:

- **The 606 Trail, Chicago, IL**: Built on a re-purposed rail line, the 606 Trail is a 2.7-mile linear park that connects diverse neighborhoods on Chicago's west side. Featuring bike paths, green spaces, and public art installations, the trail provides a space for recreation and cultural exchange, enhancing connectivity and social interaction between neighborhoods of varying socioeconomic backgrounds.

- **Via Verde, Bronx, NY**: This affordable, mixed-use housing development incorporates rooftop gardens, urban farms, and shared community spaces, all designed with social interaction and environmental sustainability in mind. Via Verde's design fosters community engagement while promoting healthy living in a densely populated, low-income neighborhood.

- **The High Line, New York City, NY**: Originally an elevated railway, the High Line has been transformed into a public park that weaves through Manhattan's West Side, incorporating art installations, accessible pathways, and native vegetation. The project actively engaged the community in its development and continues to host free public events and activities that draw diverse crowds from across the city.

- **Detroit's Eastern Market, Detroit, MI**: As one of the oldest and largest year-round markets in the U.S., Detroit's Eastern Market not only offers access to fresh food but also provides a space for community gatherings, local entrepreneurship, and cultural exchange. The market regularly hosts festivals, art exhibitions, and public events that celebrate Detroit's diverse population and history. With its focus on local food, art, and public programming, Eastern Market strengthens social bonds, supports economic resilience, and fosters a sense of community pride, making it an integral part of Detroit's social and cultural landscape.

- **Asia - Matsuzakaya Rooftop Garden, Nagoya, Japan**: This urban rooftop park combines green spaces with community areas, fostering social interaction and mental well-being in a densely populated city.

- **Europe - Superkilen Park, Copenhagen, Denmark**: This public space in a diverse neighborhood integrates elements from over 60 countries, reflecting the cultural backgrounds of its residents. The park encourages social interaction and celebrates multiculturalism, creating an inclusive, vibrant community hub.

- **The Nightingale Model, Melbourne, Australia:** The Nightingale Model is a pioneering example of socially sustainable architecture. Located in Melbourne, this series of residential projects emphasizes affordability, community, and environmental responsibility. The developments are designed with a focus on shared spaces, minimal car use, and access to green areas, fostering a strong sense of community among residents. Energy-efficient designs, rooftop solar panels, and water-saving technologies align with environmental goals, while capped developer profits ensure affordability. The Nightingale Model demonstrates how inclusive housing can address social and environmental challenges, creating vibrant, connected communities.

# #14: The Future of Sustainable Architecture

## Emerging Technologies and Innovations

Emerging technologies and innovations are reshaping the landscape of sustainable architecture, offering architects and building designers unprecedented tools to enhance both functionality and environmental responsibility in their projects. Innovations such as advanced building information modeling (BIM) facilitate the integration of sustainable practices from the initial design phase, allowing for real-time assessments of material usage, energy efficiency, and waste reduction. By utilizing these technologies, architects can create more precise models that inform decisions about layout, resource consumption, and overall project sustainability, ultimately leading to more efficient designs that align with eco-friendly principles.

In the realm of green building materials, the development of bio-based and recycled materials is transforming the construction industry. Innovations such as mycelium-based composites and recycled plastic bricks not only reduce reliance on traditional materials but also minimize the carbon footprint associated with construction. These materials often offer superior performance characteristics, such as increased insulation and durability, which enhance the energy efficiency of buildings. Architects and investors can leverage these advancements to achieve certifications like LEED or BREEAM, thereby increasing the marketability of their projects while adhering to sustainable practices.

Energy-efficient design continues to evolve with the integration of smart home technologies that enable greater control over energy consumption. Intelligent systems for heating, lighting, and appliance use allow occupants to optimize their energy usage, significantly reducing utility costs and environmental impact. Architects have the opportunity to design spaces that are not only aesthetically pleasing but also incorporate these technologies seamlessly, thus creating environments that promote energy conservation as a standard practice. This shift towards automated systems aligns with the growing consumer demand for sustainable living options, making it an essential consideration for all building projects.

Urban agriculture integration is another exciting innovation that architects can incorporate into their designs to promote sustainability in urban settings. By creating green roofs, vertical gardens, and urban farming spaces, architects can contribute to local food production while enhancing biodiversity and community well-being. These designs not only provide fresh produce but also help mitigate urban heat island effects, promote air quality, and create aesthetically pleasing environments. The inclusion of such elements in building projects can attract environmentally conscious investors and consumers, reinforcing the value of sustainability in urban development.

Finally, the principles of biophilic design are gaining traction as architects recognize the importance of connecting occupants with nature to enhance well-being and productivity. Incorporating natural materials, maximizing daylight, and creating visual connections to the outdoors not only enrich the user experience but also contribute to the overall sustainability of a building. As the industry moves towards a climate-resilient architecture framework, integrating these biophilic elements becomes essential in designing spaces that are adaptable to changing environmental conditions.

By embracing these emerging technologies and innovations, architects can lead the way toward a more sustainable future, creating buildings that are not only functional but also harmonious with their environment.

## The Role of Policy in Sustainable Practices

The role of policy in sustainable practices is pivotal in shaping the future of architecture and construction. Effective policies can drive the adoption of sustainable building practices by establishing clear guidelines and standards that promote energy efficiency, resource conservation, and environmental stewardship. Through regulatory frameworks and incentives, policymakers can encourage architects and builders to utilize green building materials, implement energy-efficient designs, and invest in technologies that reduce the carbon footprint of new developments. This alignment of policy with sustainable objectives not only enhances the viability of eco-friendly projects but also fosters a competitive market for sustainable innovations.

In many regions, policies that support sustainable practices include tax incentives, grants, and subsidies for projects that meet specific environmental criteria. These financial mechanisms can significantly lower the barriers to entry for investors and developers interested in sustainable construction. By reducing initial costs and offering financial rewards for energy-efficient designs, policies can stimulate demand for green buildings and encourage architects to prioritize sustainability in their projects. This creates a positive feedback loop where successful sustainable developments lead to further investment and policy refinement, ultimately creating a more sustainable built environment.

Furthermore, building codes and zoning regulations play a critical role in integrating sustainable practices into urban planning. Policies that mandate energy-efficient building standards, such as the Passive House standards, ensure that new constructions adhere to rigorous performance benchmarks. Additionally, urban planning policies that promote mixed-use developments can facilitate urban agriculture integration and enhance community resilience to climate change. By embedding sustainability into the fabric of urban development, policymakers enable architects and designers to create spaces that are not only functional but also environmentally harmonious.

However, the effectiveness of policies in promoting sustainable practices depends on collaboration among stakeholders. Architects, developers, and policymakers must engage in dialogue to ensure that regulations reflect the realities of construction and the needs of the community. This collaboration can lead to innovative solutions that address both environmental challenges and economic viability. By fostering partnerships between the public and private sectors, policies can be designed to encourage the adoption of smart home technologies and biophilic design principles, further enhancing the sustainability of new developments.

Ultimately, the role of policy in sustainable practices is to create a supportive framework that incentivizes innovation while ensuring accountability. By establishing clear, achievable goals for sustainability, policies can guide architects and builders toward practices that contribute to the circular economy in construction. As the built environment continues to evolve, proactive policy measures will be essential in overcoming challenges related to climate resilience and resource scarcity. In this way, policy not only shapes the architectural landscape but also plays an integral part in designing a sustainable future for communities and the planet.

# Vision for the Future of Architecture

The vision for the future of architecture is predicated on the integration of sustainable practices that redefine how we design and construct our built environments. As architects and building designers increasingly embrace sustainability, the industry is witnessing a paradigm shift toward a holistic approach that prioritizes ecological balance, resource efficiency, and community well-being. This future is characterized by the adoption of innovative materials and technologies that minimize environmental impact while enhancing the quality of life for occupants. Architects have a critical role in shaping this vision, as they are uniquely positioned to influence the built environment's sustainability trajectory through their design choices.

Incorporating green building materials is fundamental to this vision. The use of renewable resources, recycled materials, and low-impact manufacturing processes can significantly reduce a building's carbon footprint. Architects must stay informed about advances in sustainable materials, such as bio-based composites and low-VOC finishes, which contribute to healthier indoor environments. By specifying these materials, architects can help drive demand for sustainable products, encouraging manufacturers to innovate further and expand their offerings. This collaborative effort between architects and material suppliers can lead to a more sustainable construction industry, fostering a circular economy where waste is minimized, and materials are continuously repurposed.

Energy-efficient design is another cornerstone of sustainable architecture. The integration of passive design strategies, such as natural ventilation, thermal mass, and daylighting, can drastically reduce a building's energy consumption. Furthermore, the incorporation of smart home technologies enables real-time monitoring and optimization of energy use, providing occupants with tools to manage their consumption effectively. Architects should prioritize the implementation of passive house standards and energy-efficient systems in their designs, as these approaches not only enhance comfort and livability but also yield significant long-term economic benefits for investors and developers.

Urban agriculture integration is an innovative concept that aligns with sustainable urban planning principles. By incorporating green roofs, vertical gardens, and community gardens into architectural designs, architects can promote biodiversity and food security within urban settings. These features not only contribute to the aesthetic appeal of buildings but also foster community engagement and resilience against climate challenges. As cities continue to grow, the need for such integrations will become increasingly vital in ensuring that urban environments remain livable and sustainable.

Finally, biophilic design principles are essential in creating spaces that connect occupants with nature, thereby enhancing their well-being. By incorporating natural elements into architecture—such as water features, natural materials, and vegetation—designers can create environments that promote mental and physical health. Embracing these principles is vital for creating sustainable buildings that resonate with environmentally aware individuals and communities. The future of architecture lies in a collaborative effort to harmonize design with nature, fostering a sustainable legacy for generations to come.

# Vision for the Future of Architecture: 10 Key Theses

**Sustainability as Standard**: Architecture will prioritize eco-friendly materials, renewable energy systems, and circular design principles to combat climate change and reduce environmental impact.

**Resilient Design**: Buildings will be designed to withstand extreme weather events and adapt to evolving environmental conditions, ensuring long-term durability and safety.

**Integration with Nature**: Biophilic design principles will shape future architecture, fostering a deeper connection between occupants and the natural environment.

**Smart and Responsive Buildings**: AI and IoT technologies will enable buildings to dynamically adjust to occupants' needs, optimize energy use, and provide predictive maintenance.

**Urban Density and Efficiency**: Vertical cities and mixed-use developments will address urban space limitations while enhancing connectivity, efficiency, and livability.

**Cultural Preservation and Innovation**: Architecture will balance preserving historical heritage with innovative design, creating spaces that respect tradition while embracing modernity.

**Health and Well-Being**: Human-centric design will focus on improving physical and mental health through better air quality, natural light, and ergonomic spaces.

**Inclusive Design**: Future architecture will prioritize accessibility and inclusivity, creating spaces that cater to diverse needs and foster community.

**Collaboration and Community Engagement**: Architects will work closely with communities to co-create spaces that reflect local values and address societal challenges.

**Global Collaboration for Innovation**: As architecture becomes increasingly interdisciplinary, global collaboration will drive innovation, blending diverse cultural and technological perspectives.

# Conclusion on Global Architectural Trends

Worldwide, architecture is increasingly driven by sustainability, resilience, and technological innovation. The **USA** leads in smart building technologies and climate-resilient design, focusing on energy efficiency and adaptive structures. **Europe** emphasizes circular economy principles, integrating sustainability into every stage of a building's lifecycle. **Asia**, with rapid urbanization, excels in vertical cities and modular construction, blending tradition with modernity. **Australia and New Zea-**

**land** are advancing net-zero energy buildings and resilient designs tailored to diverse climates, setting regional benchmarks for sustainable practices. Meanwhile, **Africa** is making strides in low-cost, energy-efficient housing using locally sourced materials, highlighting the importance of regional solutions.

Globally, the shift towards biophilic and inclusive design reflects a shared commitment to well-being and community-focused spaces. Architects are increasingly collaborating across borders, sharing knowledge and technologies to address global challenges such as climate change and resource scarcity. The integration of AI and data-driven tools is further transforming the field, enabling more precise, efficient, and adaptive designs. These trends highlight a unified vision: creating adaptable, sustainable, and human-centered architecture for a rapidly changing world, while fostering a deep connection between people, nature, and the built environment.

About the Author: CW Wagener

Christoph Wagener holds a degree in architecture and has also completed a doctoral program in management and economics. He has considerable experience in the real estate and construction industries. He has held senior positions in joint ventures with renowned companies such as Ernst & Young, Accenture, UBS, pom+ and Drees & Sommer, and has been involved in multi-stakeholder projects of considerable scale.

He served at the University of Lucerne of Applied Sciences and Arts (HSLU) for an extended period, acting as the director of the Master of Sustainable Construction program at five Swiss universities. He currently holds a professorship in real estate and construction management at the IU University at the Freiburg Campus in Germany. His professional motto is "Transforming Real Estate through Architectural Expertise."

Designing Tomorrow: The Architect's Guide to Sustainable Building Practices

Author: CW Wagener
First Edition: November 2024
Copyright: © 2024 Christoph Wagener
Cover Design and Layout: Christoph Wagener (created by AI)
Images: Christoph Wagener (created by AI)
Publisher: Self-Published via Amazon KDP
Printing and Distribution:
Amazon ISBN-13 for paperback: 979-8300061401

Disclaimer: The contents of this book have been compiled with the utmost care. However, the author assumes no responsibility for the accuracy, completeness and timeliness of the content provided.

Imprint: Christoph Wagener % cwarc studio, 143 Pirminstrasse, Reichenau, 78479, Germany

www.ingramcontent.com/pod-product-compliance
Lightning Source LLC
Chambersburg PA
CBHW071457220526
45472CB00003B/827